Weather Watch

June

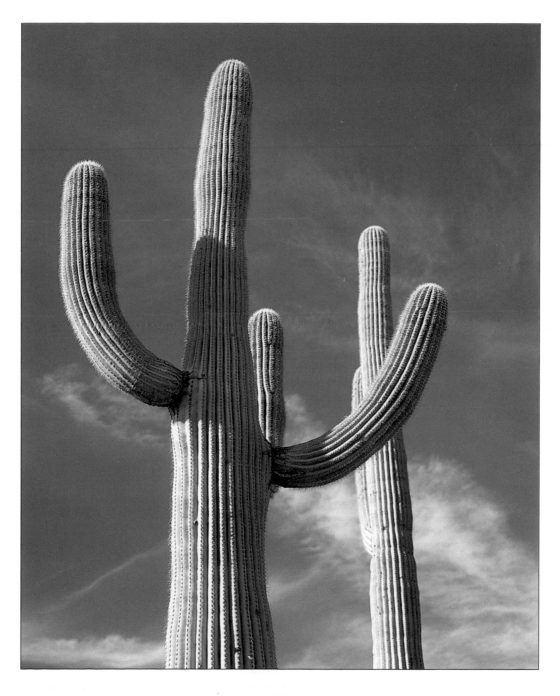

Grolier Educational

Quick reference

MAPS: This book begins with an overview of the world and then looks at each inhabited continent using the style of map shown below. These maps can be compared month by month using the other titles in the *WeatherWatch* series:

▼ This type of map shows the highest temperature that might commonly be expected in the early afternoon of any one day during the month.

You should look for patterns to see where it is warmer and colder.

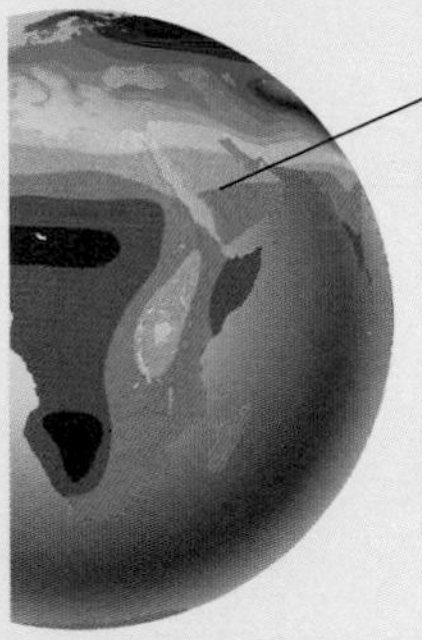

The line separating each band of color is a line of equal temperature and is called an isotherm. The key with each map shows the temperature for each isotherm. Blue to purple colors are below freezing. Green areas are up to 15°C. The yellows, oranges, and reds show the warm areas.

▼ This type of map shows the main winds, ocean currents, pressure systems, and special weather features that affect the continent during the month.

You should look at how these features might be reflected in the temperature and rainfall shown on the other maps.

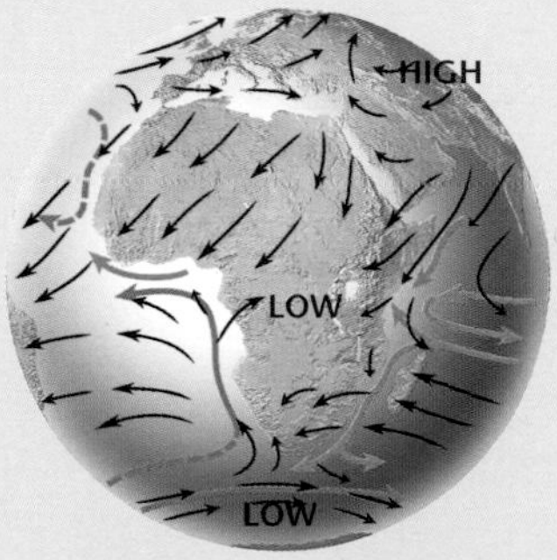
HIGH
LOW
LOW

▼ This type of map shows the average monthly temperature (°C), based on data obtained during the last 30 years. Cold temperatures are represented by the purples to blues, and warm temperatures by the yellows and reds.

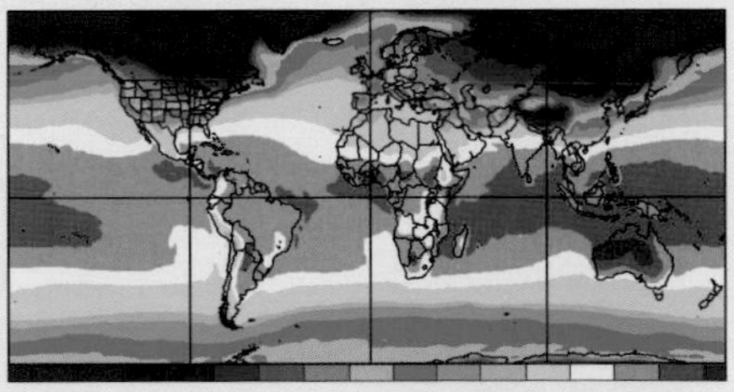

▼ This type of map shows the average monthly precipitation intensity (mm/day) (rainfall or snowfall), based on data obtained during the last 30 years. Wet areas are indicated by the purples, while dry areas are shown by the browns. See page 6 for further explanation.

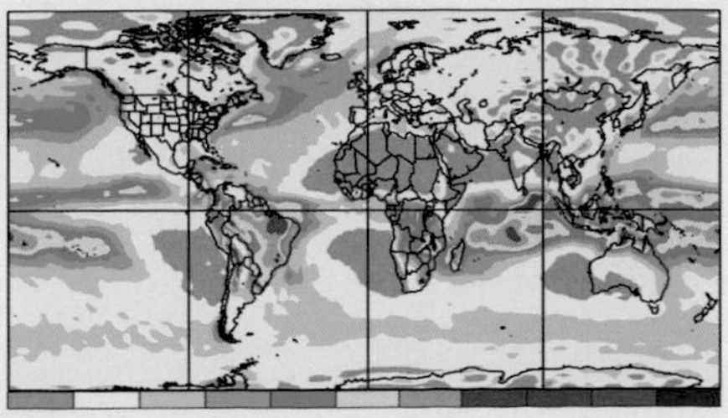

WEATHER-STATION DATA: Throughout the 12 *WeatherWatch* titles you will find monthly data for weather stations located near 72 cities around the world. The data will help you make comparisons among the cities.

City near where the weather information has been collected.

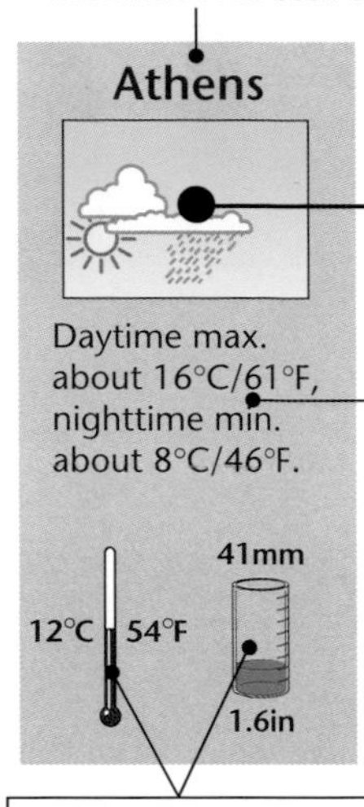
Athens
Daytime max. about 16°C/61°F, nighttime min. about 8°C/46°F.
41mm
12°C
54°F
1.6in

The expected and important weather characteristics for the month are indicated by a small picture.

Lists expected daily high (daytime) and low (nighttime) temperatures in °C and °F (it is similar to what is shown on TV and should be used only as a general guide to conditions).

Indicates the height of the sun relative to the horizon at midday.

The background color indicates the average daily temperature.

A corner bar shows when the weather is particularly uncomfortable due to windchill (blue) or heat and humidity (red).

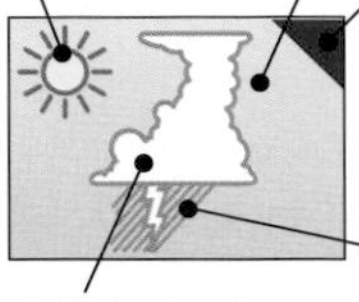

The most likely cloud types to be seen. The cloud cover is indicated by the number of cloud symbols.

Raindrops or snowflakes indicate whether there is rain or snow (precipitation). The number of these symbols suggests how much precipitation is expected.

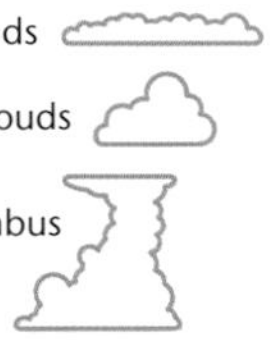

Stratus clouds

Cumulus clouds

Cumulonimbus clouds

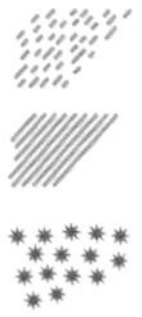

Lighter rain

Heavier rain

Snow

The average temperature (°C and °F) and precipitation (mm and inches) for the month based on long-term averages (the period of time used to compile these averages varies with the length of record at each weather station).

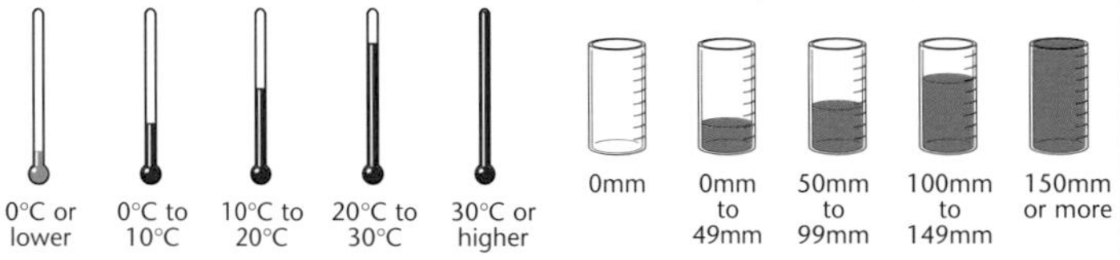
0°C or lower
0°C to 10°C
10°C to 20°C
20°C to 30°C
30°C or higher
0mm
0mm to 49mm
50mm to 99mm
100mm to 149mm
150mm or more

Where it is considered important, lightning or tornadoes are shown.

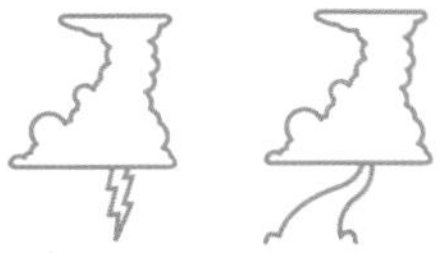

Lightning — Tornado

Cold: below 2°C/36°F average for month

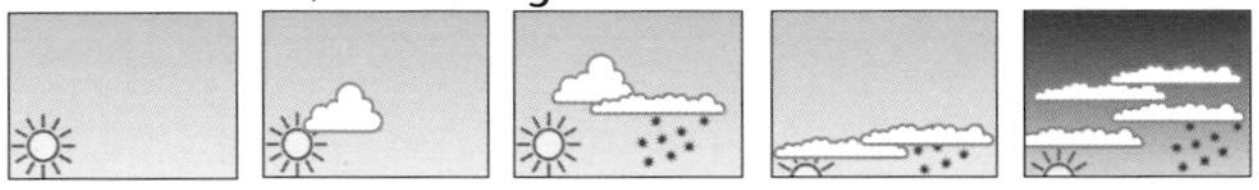

Cold sunny · Cold, fair · Cold, frontal snow showers · Cloudy, sun very low, snow · Polar twilight

Cool: between 2°C/36°F and 15°C/60°F average for month

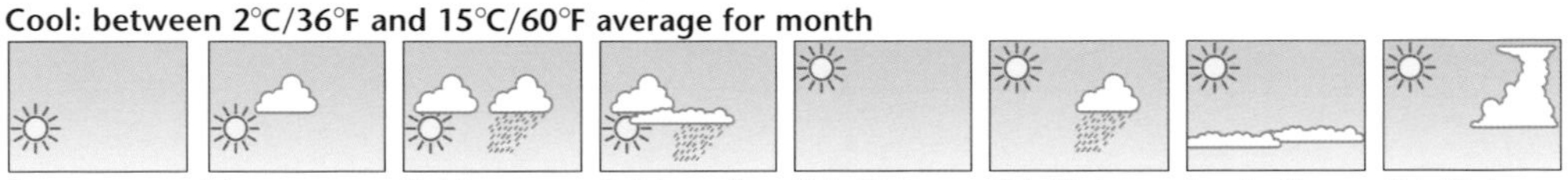

Sunny · Fair · Cool showery · Cool changeable · High-altitude sun · High-altitude showery · Low cloud/fog · High-altitude thunderstorms

Warm: between 15°C/60°F and 21°C/70°F average for month

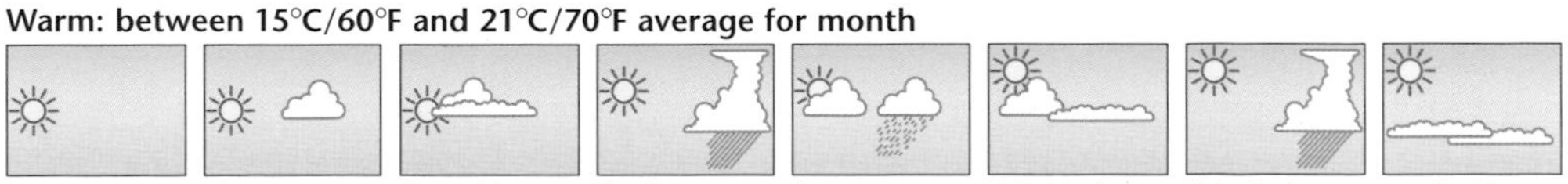

Sunny · Fair · Changeable · Thundery · Showery · High-altitude cloudy · High-altitude thundery · Low cloud/fog

Very warm: between 21°C/70°F and 27°C/80°F average for month

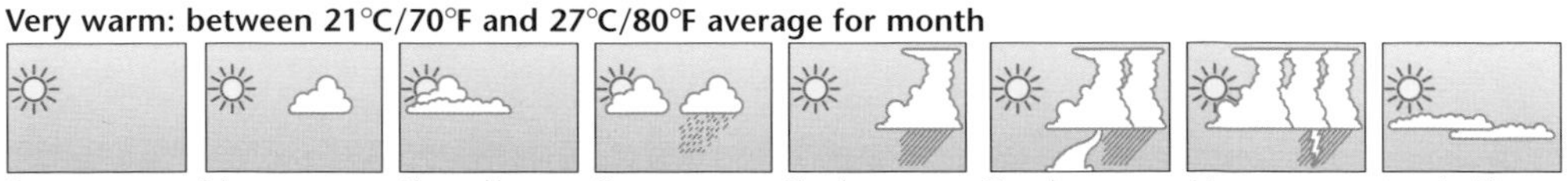

Sunny · Fair · Changeable · Showery · Thundery · Tornado · Monsoon · Low cloud/fog

Hot: 27°C/80°F to 32°C/90°F average for month

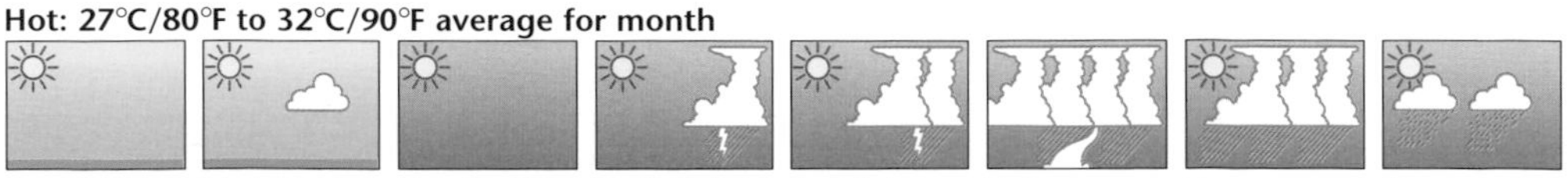

Sunny, dry air · Fair, dry air · Sunny, humid air · Humid thundery · Tropical rainstorm · Hurricane · Monsoon · Showery, humid

Very hot: over 32°C/90°F average for month

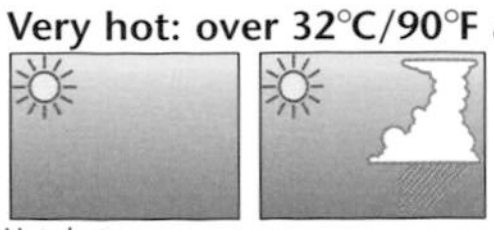

Very hot sun, brassy sky · Very hot sun, thunder (wet season)

Discomfort factors

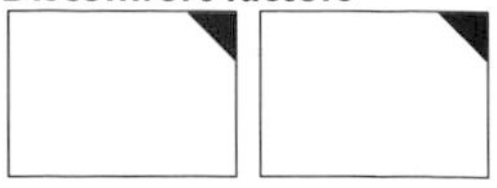

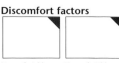

Uncomfortable because of heat or humidity · Uncomfortable because of cold or windchill

Contents

First published in the United States in 2000 by Grolier Educational, Sherman Turnpike, Danbury, CT 06816

Copyright © 2000
Atlantic Europe Publishing Company Ltd

Author
Brian Knapp, BSc, PhD
Art Director
Duncan McCrae, BSc
Editor
Mary Sanders, BSc
Page makeup and data compilation
Mark Palmer

Digital illustrations and manipulation
David Woodroffe, Duncan McCrae, Brian Knapp, and Mark Palmer
Designed and produced by
EARTHSCAPE EDITIONS
Reproduced in Malaysia by
Global Colour
Printed in Hong Kong by
Wing King Tong Company Ltd

Acknowledgments
Globes and climate maps created using base maps from Mountain High Maps® Copyright © 1993 Digital Wisdom, Inc. Maps of average surface air temperature and precipitation are adapted from the NOAA-CIRES Climatic Diagnostics Center, Boulder, Colorado.

Picture credits
All photographs are from the Earthscape Editions photolibrary except the following:
(c=center t=top b=bottom l=left r=right)
NASA 15tl; The Stock Market 25, 31

Library of Congress Cataloging-in-Publication Data
Weather watch
       p.   cm.
    Includes index.
    Contents: v. 1. January — v. 2. February — v. 3. March — v. 4. April — v. 5. May — v. 6. June — v. 7. July — v. 8. August — v. 9. September — v. 10. October — v. 11. November — v. 12. December.
Summary: Explores the basic science of weather and describes weather patterns and phenomena on the earth's continents, month by month.
ISBN 0-7172-9458-7 (set: alk. paper). — ISBN 0-7172-9459-5 (v. 1). — ISBN 0-7172-9460-9 (v. 2). — ISBN 0-7172-9461-7 (v. 3). — ISBN 0-7172-9462-5 (v. 4). — ISBN 0-7172-9463-3 (v. 5). — ISBN 0-7172-9464-1 (v. 6). — ISBN 0-7172-9465-X (v. 7). — ISBN 0-7172-9466-8 (v. 8). — ISBN 0-7172-9467-6 (v. 9). — ISBN 0-7172-9468-4 (v. 10). — ISBN 0-7172-9469-2 (v. 11). — ISBN 0-7172-9470-6 (v. 12).
    1. Climatology Juvenile literature. 2. Weather Juvenile literature [1. Climatology. 2. Weather.]
I. Grolier Educational Corporation.
QC981.3.W428 1999
551.6 — dc21   99-34566
                            CIP

This product is manufactured from sustainable managed forests. For every tree cut down, at least one more is planted.

The world in June

During June the monsoon begins in many parts of the northern hemisphere. By contrast, tropical lands south of the equator mainly experience a dry season, while the southern midlatitudes continue to be cool and unsettled.

The WEATHER is a combination of sunshine and cloud, dampness (HUMIDITY), rain or snow (PRECIPITATION), wind and calm, and warmth and cold (TEMPERATURE) on a particular day.

Depending on where you are, one day may be very much like the next, or it may change greatly. But over the years the day-to-day weather forms a recognizable pattern called the CLIMATE. In this book you will find the expected patterns of weather across the world during June.

Why the weather varies across the world

Weather patterns over the earth are produced because the sun heats the earth more in some places than others. Whenever the land or the ocean becomes warm, it shares its heat with the air above. This warmed air then expands, becomes less heavy, and rises, leaving room for more air to flow in to take its place. Whenever the land or ocean is cold, the air touching it loses heat and cools down, becomes more dense, sinks, and spreads out.

In these ways the air begins to circulate. The CIRCULATION is felt as winds. Because it is generally warmer in the TROPICS than at the poles, the circulation of air involves the whole lower ATMOSPHERE.

Air also flows between places where the AIR PRESSURE is lower than average (low-pressure areas, called LOWS) and places where the air pressure is higher than average (high-pressure areas, called HIGHS).

The pattern in the tropics

The world's biggest low is caused by hot air rising near the equator (it is called the EQUATORIAL LOW). Its position moves north and south during the year as it follows the movement of the

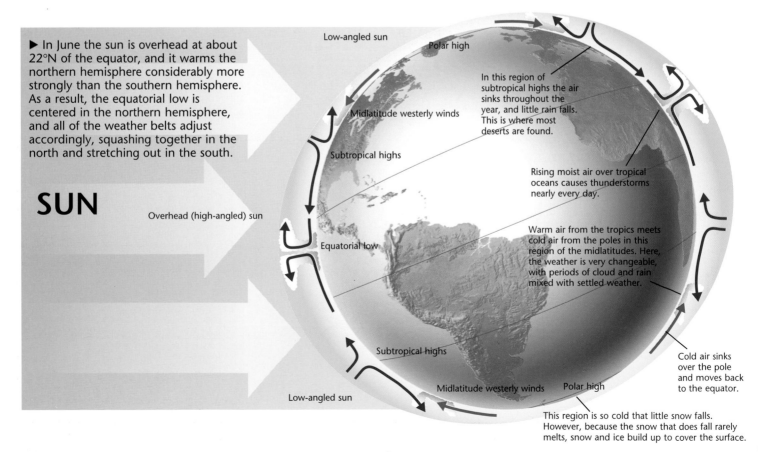

▶ In June the sun is overhead at about 22°N of the equator, and it warms the northern hemisphere considerably more strongly than the southern hemisphere. As a result, the equatorial low is centered in the northern hemisphere, and all of the weather belts adjust accordingly, squashing together in the north and stretching out in the south.

SUN

Low-angled sun

Polar high

Midlatitude westerly winds

Subtropical highs

Overhead (high-angled) sun

Equatorial low

In this region of subtropical highs the air sinks throughout the year, and little rain falls. This is where most deserts are found.

Rising moist air over tropical oceans causes thunderstorms nearly every day.

Warm air from the tropics meets cold air from the poles in this region of the midlatitudes. Here, the weather is very changeable, with periods of cloud and rain mixed with settled weather.

Subtropical highs

Midlatitude westerly winds

Polar high

Low-angled sun

Cold air sinks over the pole and moves back to the equator.

This region is so cold that little snow falls. However, because the snow that does fall rarely melts, snow and ice build up to cover the surface.

▼ This map shows the earth's main climate types. Notice how they fall mainly in bands parallel to the equator. Mountains and other special features break up this pattern. Each climate is fully described in the Glossary that begins on page 44.

Hot climates
- Equatorial and tropical marine
- Tropical continental and monsoon

Dry climates
- Hot with seasonal rain
- Cool with dry winter
- Desert

Warm subtropical or temperate climates
- Dry winter
- Rain throughout year
- Dry summer

Cool temperate climates
- Marine
- Continental

Cold climates
- Continental

Polar and mountain climates
- Arctic
- Ice
- Mountain

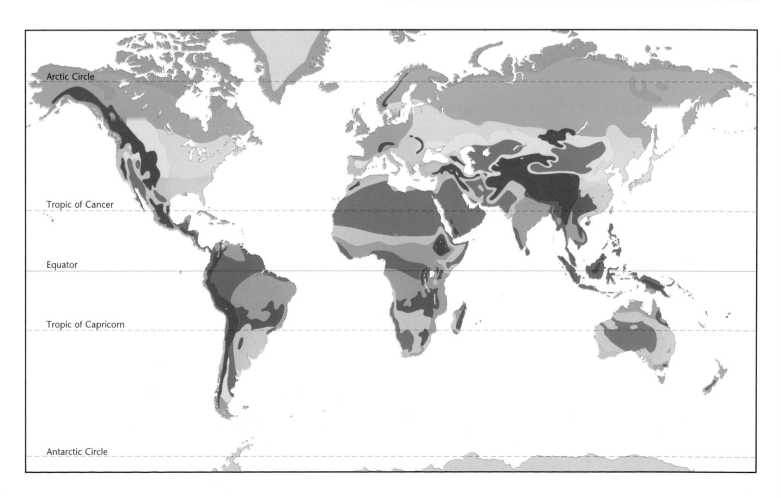

Arctic Circle

Tropic of Cancer

Equator

Tropic of Capricorn

Antarctic Circle

OVERHEAD SUN (see page 4) and the latitude of greatest heating. The equatorial low is the heat "engine" that powers the entire global circulation. Cloud and rain are produced by rising air, making the equatorial low also the world's main rain-producing area and the place of the great tropical rainforests.

With air rising near the equator, air has to sink elsewhere to keep the atmosphere in balance. This happens at about latitude 30°–35° in each hemisphere. The sinking air creates high-pressure regions (known as SUBTROPICAL HIGHS). In this sinking air cloud cannot form, and it is nearly always dry. Here lie many of the world's great DESERTS.

Air continually flows from the subtropical highs to the equatorial low. This creates the TRADE WINDS.

The position of the equatorial low and subtropical highs changes in a very predictable way during the year and gives places in the tropics very predictable seasons: wet when the equatorial low is nearby and dry when the band of subtropical highs is close. The tropics are hot throughout the year.

The pattern in the midlatitudes

The MIDLATITUDES are the regions between the tropics and the Arctic or Antarctic. Here the winds flow from west to east very quickly (forming the PREVAILING WESTERLY WINDS), and just as in a fast-flowing river, disturbances, or eddies, are an important feature.

A downward-spiraling eddy produces a temporary high (known as an ANTICYCLONE) with settled weather; an upward-spiraling eddy produces a temporary low (called a DEPRESSION) with unsettled weather. These anticyclones and depressions form and re-form, shifting position as they are carried along by the westerly winds (westerlies). Lows, in particular, draw in air first from the tropics and then from the poles. This is why the midlatitudes have the most changeable weather in the world.

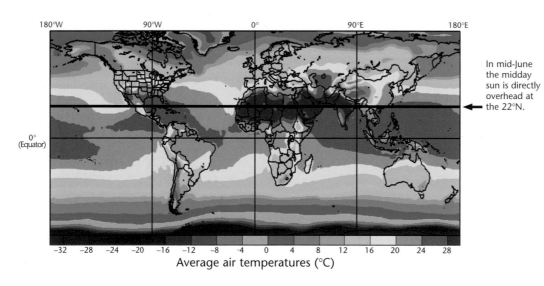

In mid-June the midday sun is directly overhead at the 22°N.

Average air temperatures (°C)

◄ This map shows the pattern of temperature for the month, averaged over the last 30 years. The blues and purples show below-freezing temperatures, the greens show cool to mild temperatures, the yellows are warm, oranges very warm, and the reds show hot to very hot. These colors are the same as those used on all the temperature maps in this book. The scale used is the Celsius scale and marked in °C. The equator and lines of longitude at 90° intervals are also shown.

► This map shows the pattern of precipitation for the month, averaged over the last 30 years. The browns show where the average precipitation has been very low. The yellows show light, the greens moderate, and the blues heavy. The purples show very heavy precipitation, often connected to monsoons, hurricanes, or frequent thunderstorms. The metric millimeter scale is marked in mm/day. Multiply by 31 to find the average precipitation for the month (e.g., 3mm/day = 93mm, or 3.7 inches, for the month). The equator and lines of longitude at 90° intervals are also shown.

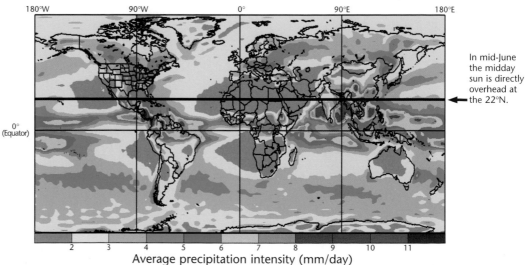

In mid-June the midday sun is directly overhead at the 22°N.

Average precipitation intensity (mm/day)

The effect of the great continents

Lows and highs can also be formed by heat and cold. It gets very hot over the centers of large continents each summer because they are far from the cooling effects of the oceans. These continents are therefore places where the hot air rises, and thus where seasonal lows form. The summer lows draw in moist air from the nearby oceans and produce thundery rainstorms.

The same places get very cold in the winter and form seasonal highs. Winter highs are associated with mostly dry weather. These changing highs and lows add to the complexity of weather and may give rise to MONSOONS.

JUNE

June is the midpoint of the weather year.

The overhead sun is at its farthest north, but the land, and even more so, the oceans, take time to soak up the heat they are receiving, and only when they have done so do they share this heat with the air. As a result, June is still early summer and not the hottest month in the north; nor is it midwinter, nor the coldest month in the south. They will occur in July.

The tropics north of the equator are experiencing the onset of the monsoon, while those to the south are enjoying the dry season. This is one of the least wet times of the year close to the equator.

The hottest part of the world lies between the Sahara Desert and India.

WEATHER HAZARD: FLASH FLOODS

Flash floods are produced by local thunderstorms in barren, mountainous terrain. A torrential thunderstorm may release water very quickly. If the rain falls onto steep-sided slopes without soil, the water will run off quickly and begin to fill up the valley bottom before it has a chance to run away. The water picks up sand, silt, and other debris from the valley floor as it surges forward, and this turns the water into something like liquid cement. The result is that the flow of water slows down and gives time for more water to flood into the valley bottom.

All the time the flood is moving, the clear water from behind pours over the top of the water at the front and, in turn, becomes a mixture of sediment and water. Within minutes a wall of water and sediment can be moving at the speed of an express train through a valley. The local nature of the storm means that people farther down the valley may be completely unaware that there is any danger. Many people have been killed in mountainous desert terrain by such flash floods.

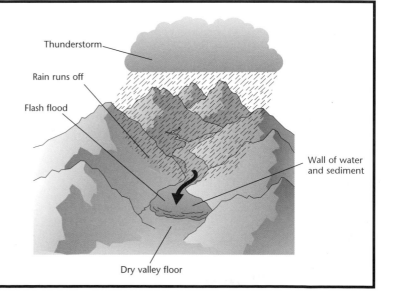

Thunderstorm

Rain runs off

Flash flood

Wall of water and sediment

Dry valley floor

North America

The peak time for summer vacations begins this month, and many Americans use the Memorial Day holiday as a signal to start weekend trips in earnest. In fact, June is one of the sunniest months in the north and east, but there are more thunderstorms to watch out for in the west and south.

The weather in June is influenced by the height of the midday sun, the length of the days, and also by the location of the great centers of high pressure off the coasts.

This month sees the longest days of the year, with the sun highest in the sky. The warmth of the sun means that the cold high-pressure center of winter has been replaced by a warm low-pressure region that covers much of the interior of the continent. The clear skies and high-angled sun mean that the land heats up rapidly each day. Although much of the heat is lost, some of it is stored in the soil, making the

▼ This map shows the highest temperatures expected during June. Use it to imagine what conditions are like in the early afternoon.

There is a remarkable evenness of daytime temperatures in June, and the map shows few color changes. There are two reasons for this: first, the northern parts of the continent have warmed up, and second, the southern part of the continent is experiencing more by way of thunderstorms, whose cloud and rain hold down daytime temperatures. (The average temperatures for North America in June, which include the effect of cold nights, are shown on the map on page 10.)

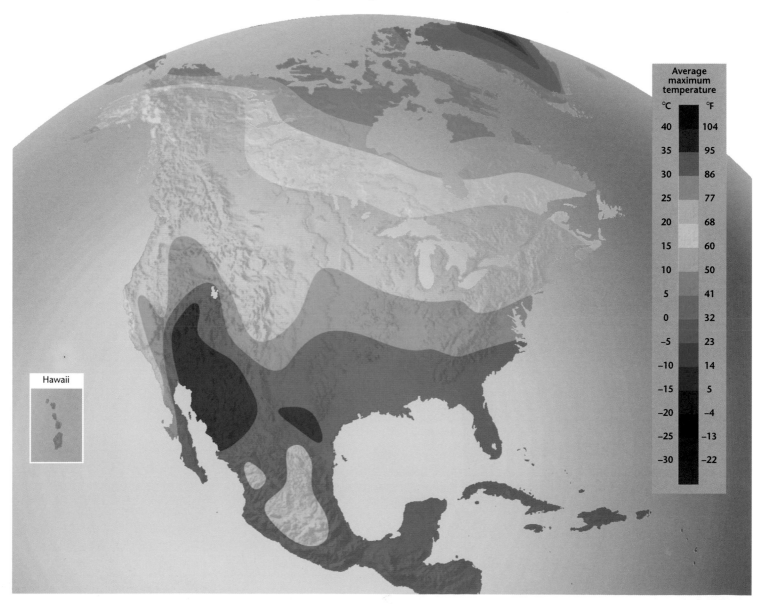

Average maximum temperature	
°C	°F
40	104
35	95
30	86
25	77
20	68
15	60
10	50
5	41
0	32
−5	23
−10	14
−15	5
−20	−4
−25	−13
−30	−22

Hawaii

next day slightly warmer. The much longer days of the north partly compensate for the lower angle of the sun, and this helps explain why there is much less difference between the highest temperatures in the north and the south of the continent than has been the case for many months.

The high in the east Pacific now dominates the weather over California, deflecting any westerly winds to the north. In June northern California and Oregon are sunny, and even the coasts of Washington and British Columbia can look forward to long, sunny dry spells.

The heating of the interior of the continent pulls in warm, moist air from the Gulf of Mexico. The subtropical jet stream is high over the southern part of the United States, in part steering the moist air from the Gulf in a northeasterly direction toward the Gulf Atlantic states and away from western Texas. That is why this is a month when the whole southeast of the United States can expect to be thoroughly drenched by thunderstorms.

The hot days and moist air from the Gulf are a combination guaranteed to produce humid, uncomfortably sticky weather, with the risk of giant thunderstorms and tornadoes ever present. Tornado watches are active in a broad band of the country from Texas to the Carolinas, while thunderstorms are likely to disrupt air traffic in and out of the Midwest airports and all along the Front Range just east of the Rocky Mountains. In fact, the cloud produced by the rising hot air tends to make days in the south less sunny than in the north, and this caps the amount of heat received. Nevertheless, this is just the weather that corn needs for growing and for the cobs to swell, and this explains why the Midwest is the corn capital of the world.

▲ Photochemical smog produced by anticyclonic conditions over Los Angeles.

▲ Clear, sunny skies of the Arizona desert near Flagstaff.

◄ Thunderclouds developing behind geyers in Yellowstone National Park, Wyoming.

Some of the warm Gulf air even takes a curving, northeasterly path to sweep up as far as Canada, bringing a welcome increase in rain to Manitoba and other prairie provinces.

In the northern Pacific Ocean the Aleutian low is still steering westerly winds across the northern part of the continent, and depressions pass from the west to the east coast. However, they travel by a quite northerly route, so that much of the United States is clear. You can see this by the greatly increased amount of sunshine in Seattle. The Rocky Mountains act as a further barrier to the westerly winds.

Although June is not yet the hottest month of the year, temperatures are soaring in the southwest, for example, in the Phoenix region, where the moist Gulf air does not reach. California is also warm and sunny, with the fogs of San Francisco only now starting to roll in over the coast.

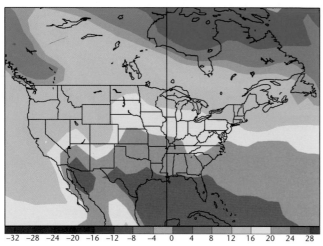

−32 −28 −24 −20 −16 −12 −8 −4 0 4 8 12 16 20 24 28

▲ This map shows the average air temperature over North America (°C) in June.

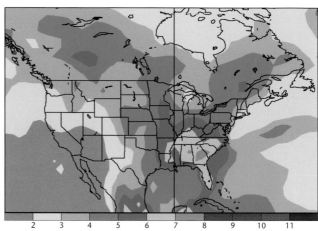

2   3   4   5   6   7   8   9   10   11

▲ This map shows the average amount of precipitation that falls over North America (in mm/day) in June.

▼ This map shows the main weather systems and ocean currents in June.

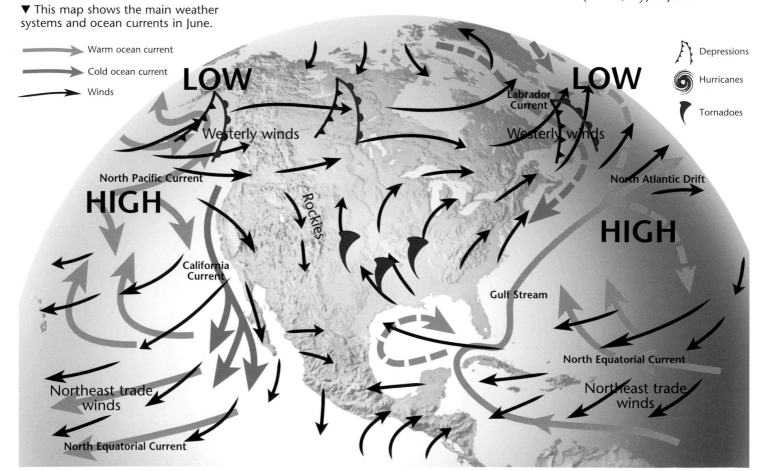

Warm ocean current
Cold ocean current
Winds

LOW
Westerly winds
North Pacific Current
HIGH
California Current
Rockies
Northeast trade winds
North Equatorial Current

Labrador Current
LOW
Westerly winds
North Atlantic Drift
HIGH
Gulf Stream
North Equatorial Current
Northeast trade winds

Depressions
Hurricanes
Tornadoes

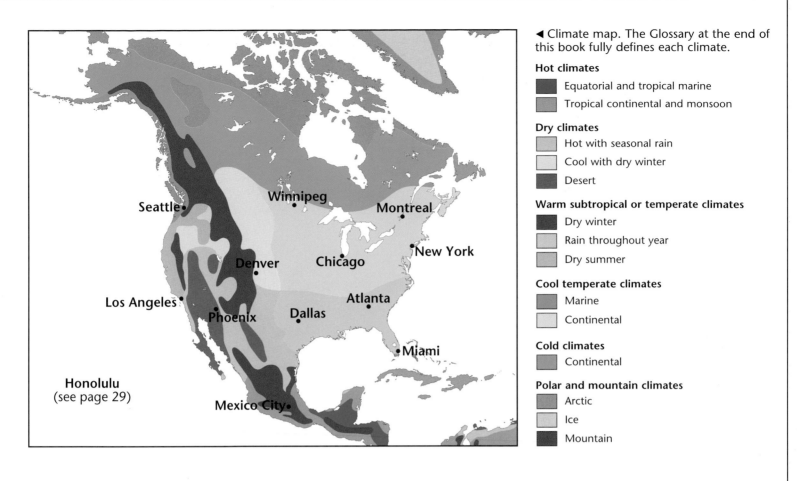

◄ Climate map. The Glossary at the end of this book fully defines each climate.

Hot climates
- Equatorial and tropical marine
- Tropical continental and monsoon

Dry climates
- Hot with seasonal rain
- Cool with dry winter
- Desert

Warm subtropical or temperate climates
- Dry winter
- Rain throughout year
- Dry summer

Cool temperate climates
- Marine
- Continental

Cold climates
- Continental

Polar and mountain climates
- Arctic
- Ice
- Mountain

Seattle • Winnipeg • Montreal • New York • Chicago • Denver • Atlanta • Los Angeles • Phoenix • Dallas • Miami • Mexico City •

Honolulu (see page 29)

Atlanta

Daytime max. about 30°C/86°F, nighttime min. about 19°C/66°F

92mm
24°C | 75°F
3.6in

Chicago

Daytime max. about 24°C/75°F, nighttime min. about 16°C/61°F

101mm
21°C | 70°F
4.0in

Dallas

Daytime max. about 32°C/90°F, nighttime min. about 22°C/72°F

86mm
28°C | 82°F
3.4in

Denver

Daytime max. about 23°C/73°F, nighttime min. about 8°C/46°F

50mm
19°C | 66°F
2.0in

Los Angeles

Daytime max. about 24°C/75°F, nighttime min. about 13°C/55°F

1.2mm
18°C | 64°F
0.0in

Mexico City

Daytime max. about 24°C/75°F, nighttime min. about 13°C/55°F

106mm
18°C | 64°F
4.2in

Miami

Daytime max. about 30°C/86°F, nighttime min. about 23°C/73°F

173mm
27°C | 81°F
6.8in

Montreal

Daytime max. about 24°C/75°F, nighttime min. about 12°C/54°F

90mm
19°C | 66°F
3.6in

New York

Daytime max. about 25°C/77°F, nighttime min. about 16°C/61°F

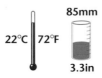
85mm
22°C | 72°F
3.3in

Phoenix

Daytime max. about 38°C/100°F, nighttime min. about 21°C/70°F

2.7mm
28°C | 82°F
0.1in

Seattle

Daytime max. about 21°C/70°F, nighttime min. about 11°C/52°F

37mm
16°C | 61°F
1.5in

Winnipeg

Daytime max. about 23°C/73°F, nighttime min. about 10°C/50°F

81mm
17°C | 63°F
3.2in

See the Quick reference on page 2 for an explanation of the symbols used here.

Chicago

Chicago, known as the windy city, has a climate of contrasts. It is extremely cold in winter, hot and sticky in summer, with thunderstorms that peak in June. But it is also a city of sunshine.

STATION: Chicago, Illinois, is located at about 41.78°N 87.60°W. Height about 200m/600ft above sea level.

CLIMATE: Cool temperate, continental climate.

Chicago – nicknamed "the windy city" – lies on the Great Plains near the southern end of Lake Michigan. Its climate is mainly continental because it is close to the heart of the North American continent, but the presence of the Great Lakes strongly affects the city.

Chicago lies in the path of the westerly winds that affect much of the northern part of North America. However, although depressions are carried across Chicago on the westerly winds, by the time they reach the city, they have passed over so much land that they have shed much of their moisture. The bonus is that Chicago is sunnier than many other cities at the same latitude, for example, New York.

Winters are harsh in Chicago. This is because a large pool of cold air, whose center is to the north of Hudson Bay, spreads over the Great Lakes and beyond Chicago. It turns the ground as hard as iron.

Whenever westerly winds do penetrate across Chicago, they bring bitingly cold winds. There is nothing on the flat, open landscape to provide shelter. These winds, if combined with snow, can cause blizzards.

Because the air is so cold, it can hold little moisture, and so winter is the driest time of the year. So, although snow falls, it is not usually

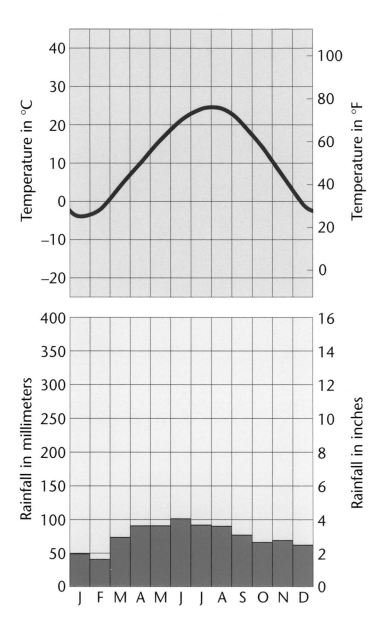

| | JANUARY | FEBRUARY | MARCH | APRIL | MAY | JUNE |

deep. Nevertheless, with temperatures staying below freezing for several months, snow does not melt but stays piled up on the roadsides, and icicles hang from buildings. Heating systems are at full blast day and night.

During spring the winter high is replaced by a region of warm air. This air rises, forming a low-pressure center that helps suck moist, warm air northward from the Gulf of Mexico.

During summer the clear early morning skies allow the sun to heat the land and set off CONVECTIONAL activity. Massive thunderstorms can occur by midafternoon, making summer the season when most rain falls. Flights in and out of Chicago O'Hare Airport are frequently disrupted by such storms.

Summer is also a time when the air is hot and humid, and heating systems are replaced by air-conditioners. However, while much of the city is hot and sticky, a "sea breeze" builds up along the shore of Lake Michigan, making shoreline conditions much more pleasant than the rest of the city. It also makes the lakeside the most desirable location for a home.

The Chicago area is ideal cereal-growing country because the rain falls in the early growing season when it is most needed, and hot summer temperatures allow the crops to ripen easily.

▲ Chicago, the windy city, lies at the eastern end of the prairies. There is no shelter here. In summer a lake breeze makes the lakeside apartments and houses the most desirable.

	Jan	Feb	Mar	Apr	May	Jun	Jul	Aug	Sep	Oct	Nov	Dec	Year
Average daily temperature													
°C	–4	–2	4	10	16	21	24	24	20	14	6	–1	**11**
°F	25	28	39	50	61	70	75	75	68	57	43	30	**52**
Average rainfall per month													
mm	49	41	73	92	92	101	93	91	77	66	69	62	**906**
ins	1.9	1.6	2.9	3.6	3.6	4.0	3.7	3.6	3.0	2.6	2.7	2.4	**35.7**
Average sunshine per day													
hrs	4	5	7	7	9	10	10	9	8	7	5	4	**7**

JULY	AUGUST	SEPTEMBER	OCTOBER	NOVEMBER	DECEMBER

South America

June is a cool, cloudy, and wintery time of year in the far south. Near the equator it is still the rainy season, and torrential rain falls. But for the bulk of the continent it is one of the drier months of the year.

Midwinter has arrived in the south of South America, and the days are at their shortest. It is not yet the coldest time of the year – that will be next month. In any case, because South America reaches only about as far south as Scotland is north of the equator, for the bulk of the continent it is a cool, not a cold time of the year. Furthermore, because the southern part of the continent is so narrow, the influence of the oceans has an important effect in helping keep temperatures up. The only place that is truly cold is along the spine of the high Andes Mountains, and by June they are already deeply snow covered, and there is little more precipitation.

The main changes that take place during winter occur in the south. By June the two great areas of

▼ This map shows the highest temperatures expected during June. Use it to imagine what conditions are like in the early afternoon.

The daytime warmth of the Amazon Basin is still holding on, helped by the warmth of the ocean current that washes onto the coast of northern Brazil and the Caribbean. However, most places to the south are now cool. The mountain backbone of the Andes is cool everywhere. (The average temperatures for South America in June, which include the effect of cold nights, are shown on the map on page 16.)

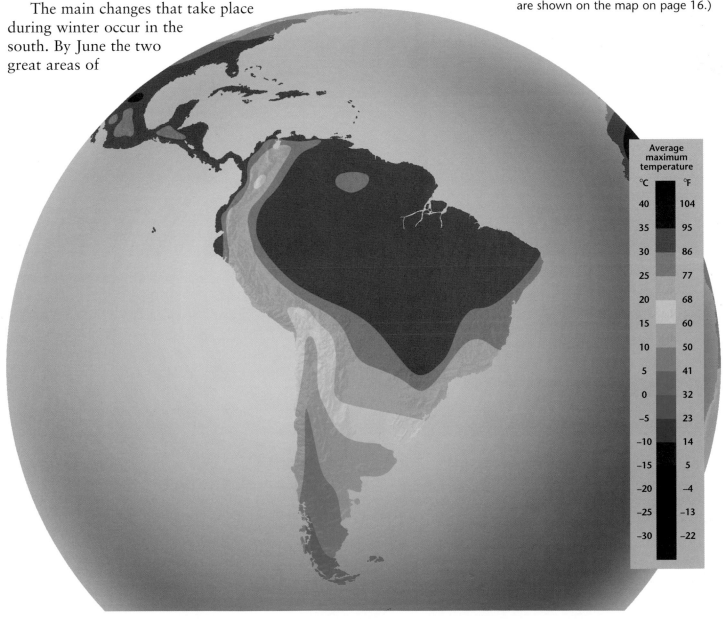

Average maximum temperature	
°C	°F
40	104
35	95
30	86
25	77
20	68
15	60
10	50
5	41
0	32
–5	23
–10	14
–15	5
–20	–4
–25	–13
–30	–22

However with low pressure following the overhead sun toward the north of the continent, conditions in the north are very different. Furthermore, the warm ocean waters crossing the Atlantic are now washing the shores of northern Brazil and flowing into the Caribbean. The air is therefore hot and filled with moisture. This is the start of a particularly sticky and oppressive time of year. The result is that a band of thundery rain straddles northern Brazil, Venezuela, and the Caribbean. Kingston in Jamaica has 96mm/3.8in of rain in June and Caracas 104mm/4.1in, while Belém in northeastern Brazil has 164mm/6.5in.

◀ South America and the Pacific Ocean as seen from space. The swirling bands of cloud mark depressions that are bringing more changeable conditions to the southern parts the continent. Cloud is associated with thunderstorms in the Amazon Basin. The westward flow of air is blocked by the spine of the high Andes Mountains. Like the Andes, the deserts of the western coast are free of clouds. The coastal fog banks that lie over the Peruvian Current can be seen close to the coasts of northern Chile and Peru.

▼ Cloudless skies over the Atacama Desert on the western seaboard of South America. It is not surprising that this is one of the driest places on earth. It is believed that parts of this desert have not had rain for centuries.

subtropical high pressure have moved nearly as far toward the equator as they will go. This allows the westerly winds to spread north, and in June they influence the continent from the southern tip to central Chile.

Unsettled weather and periods of rain are now common both in Santiago (and its port Valparaiso) in Chile on the west coast and Buenos Aires in Argentina on the east. In fact, the place in the south with the greatest rainfall this month is not Tierra del Fuego on the southern tip of South America (Punta Arenas has 32mm/1.3in) but Valparaiso (which has 90mm/3.5in).

The cooling down of the southern part of the continent means that pressure is high enough to keep down the amount of thunderstorm rain. The result is to make June one of the driest months in South America south of the Amazon.

All of these changes have not, however, had any effect on the coastal deserts of Peru and Chile, for here, where the Pacific Ocean high remains offshore all year long, winds still blow offshore, and no rain falls.

The ancient Inca calendar marked June as the most important month since it sees the winter solstice (shortest day in the southern hemisphere). The ceremony marking the solstice in Cuzco, Peru, is the most spectacular, with the events held in the vast stone fortress of Sacsahuaman. The ceremonies always end before the chilly mountain night arrives.

In the much warmer climates of the Caribbean, Barbados is beginning to party in a celebration called Crop Over. It commemorates the days when the slaves working on the plantations finally finished the harvest after four months of backbreaking work in the dry season.

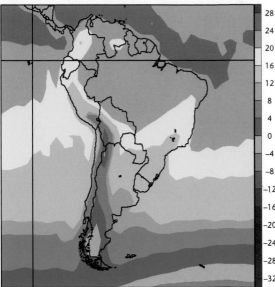

▼ This map shows the average air temperature over South America (°C) in June.

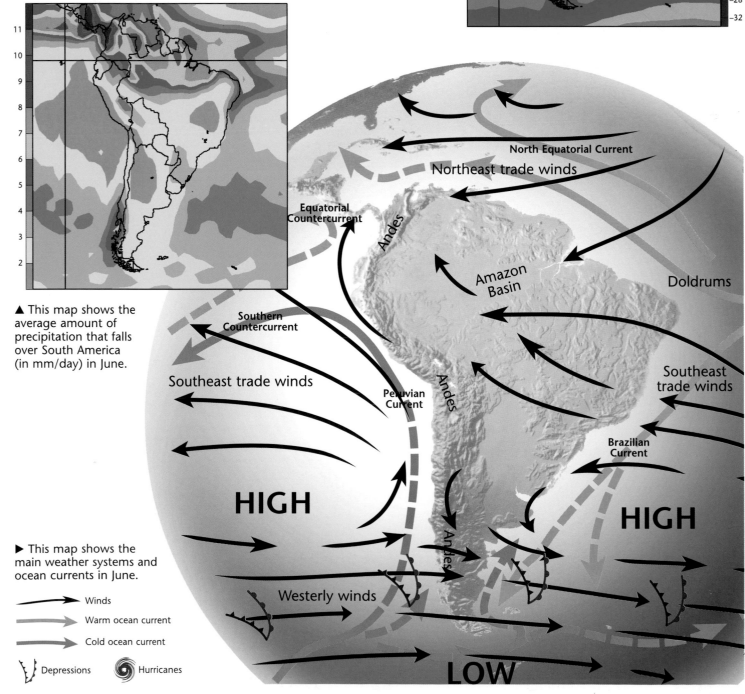

▲ This map shows the average amount of precipitation that falls over South America (in mm/day) in June.

► This map shows the main weather systems and ocean currents in June.

North Equatorial Current

Northeast trade winds

Equatorial Countercurrent

Andes

Amazon Basin

Doldrums

Southern Countercurrent

Southeast trade winds

Peruvian Current

Andes

Southeast trade winds

Brazilian Current

HIGH

Andes

HIGH

Westerly winds

LOW

Winds

Warm ocean current

Cold ocean current

Depressions

Hurricanes

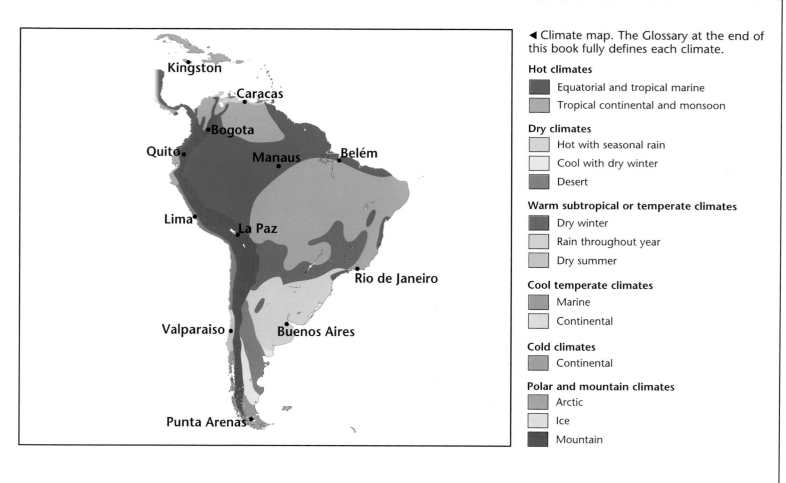

◀ Climate map. The Glossary at the end of this book fully defines each climate.

Hot climates
- Equatorial and tropical marine
- Tropical continental and monsoon

Dry climates
- Hot with seasonal rain
- Cool with dry winter
- Desert

Warm subtropical or temperate climates
- Dry winter
- Rain throughout year
- Dry summer

Cool temperate climates
- Marine
- Continental

Cold climates
- Continental

Polar and mountain climates
- Arctic
- Ice
- Mountain

Belém

Daytime max. about 31°C/88°F, nighttime min. about 22°C/72°F

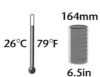
26°C | 79°F | 164mm | 6.5in

Bogota

Daytime max. about 18°C/64°F, nighttime min. about 11°C/52°F

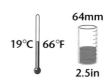
19°C | 66°F | 64mm | 2.5in

Buenos Aires

Daytime max. about 14°C/57°F, nighttime min. about 5°C/41°F

10°C | 50°F | 64mm | 2.5in

Caracas

Daytime max. about 26°C/79°F, nighttime min. about 17°C/63°F

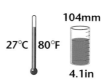
27°C | 80°F | 104mm | 4.1in

Kingston

Daytime max. about 32°C/90°F, nighttime min. about 23°C/73°F

28°C | 82°F | 96mm | 3.8in

La Paz

Daytime max. about 17°C/63°F, nighttime min. about 1°C/34°F

7°C | 45°F | 6.1mm | 0.2in

Lima

Daytime max. about 20°C/68°F, nighttime min. about 14°C/57°F

17°C | 63°F | 1.8mm | 0.1in

Manaus

Daytime max. about 31°C/88°F, nighttime min. about 24°C/75°F

26°C | 79°F | 103mm | 4.1in

Punta Arenas

Daytime max. about 5°C/41°F, nighttime min. about 1°C/34°F

2°C | 36°F | 32mm | 1.3in

Quito

Daytime max. about 22°C/72°F, nighttime min. about 7°C/45°F

13°C | 55°F | 48mm | 1.9in

Rio de Janeiro

Daytime max. about 24°C/75°F, nighttime min. about 18°C/64°F

21°C | 70°F | 52mm | 2.0in

Valparaiso

Daytime max. about 14°C/57°F, nighttime min. about 3°C/37°F

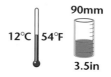
12°C | 54°F | 90mm | 3.5in

See the Quick reference on page 2 for an explanation of the symbols used here.

Bogota

Bogota has a tropical pattern of wet and dry seasons, and much of its rain is from true tropical thunderstorms. But its higher altitude means the air is clear and as cool as in the midlatitudes. June marks the start of the drier part of the year.

STATION: Bogota, Columbia, is located at about 4.34°N 74.40°W. Height about 1,550m/5,085ft above sea level.

CLIMATE: Equatorial high-altitude climate.

Bogota lies in one of the wide valleys among the Andes Mountains of Colombia. High-altitude climates on the equator still have the year-round evenness of temperature that you find at low altitudes close to the equator, but the higher altitude results in lower temperatures. As you go up by 100m/330ft, the temperature goes down by about 0.5°C/1°F. So, for example, many high mountain places have a temperature more like a midlatitude summer all year round. As a result, Bogota has a warm climate (about 19°C/67°F throughout the year), not a hot one, as would be the case near sea level. In South America, where many cities are found at high altitude, this kind of location is called *terra fria* (cool land).

The temperature conditions provide a more comfortable working climate than in the lowlands. This is why Bogota was the preferred choice as a capital city by the former Spanish colonists and why the modern government stays there. As a result, in Colombia government is located in the *terra fria*, while industry, ports, and farming (which need to be where the soils are more fertile and the transportation better) are on the nearby hot and steamy coasts.

Bogota has an even greater degree of evenness to its average temperatures than places in the lowlands. The temperature

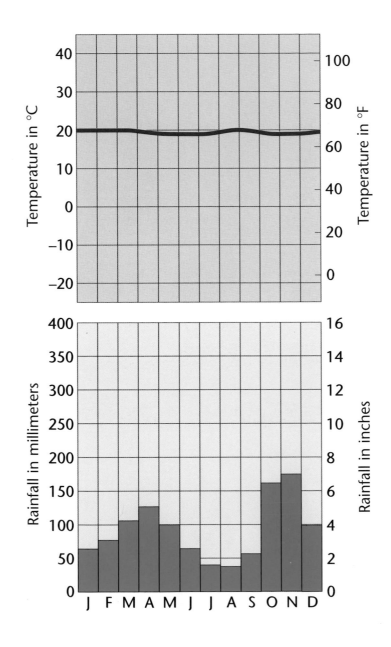

between months in Bogota varies by less than 1°C/2°F. On the other hand, the daily (diurnal) range is immense, ranging over 15–20°C/27–36°F, and frost is common at night. Even more strangely for a city on the equator, much of the precipitation is in the form of sleet or snow!

The rarefied air does not hinder incoming sunshine or outgoing heat. Unless you have experienced being in such a place, it is hard to imagine the result: walk out of the hot sunshine and into the shade of a building, and you will immediately feel freezing cold. Also, without dust and moisture the air cannot disperse the sunlight, so that the sun is intensely bright. Shadows are similarly intensely dark and quite unlike those found elsewhere in the world.

And the aspect of a slope (the direction it faces and therefore how much sun it catches) is not as important as it would be, for example, in the Alps or Himalaya Mountains because the midday sun is directly overhead each day and is never at the more extreme angles it reaches at higher latitudes.

Rainfall follows the equatorial pattern, with two periods of highest rainfall centered around April and November. But because Bogota is high,

the cooler air holds less moisture, and the city is much drier than places close to sea level.

Rainfall comes from CONVECTIONAL THUNDERSTORMS, so each day tends to start sunny clear and cold, then it soon warms up to produce a pleasant morning. Clouds build up during the morning, and rain falls in the midafternoon.

A similar pattern of rainfall and temperature is found in other equatorial cities in the Andes. See, for example, Quito, Ecuador, in the November volume.

▲ Bogota now sprawls over the valley floor among the high Andes.

	Jan	Feb	Mar	Apr	May	Jun	Jul	Aug	Sep	Oct	Nov	Dec	Year
Average daily temperature													
°C	20	20	20	19	19	19	19	20	20	19	19	19	**19**
°F	68	68	68	66	66	66	66	68	68	66	66	66	**66**
Average rainfall per month													
mm	64	77	106	126	100	64	41	38	57	162	174	98	**1,107**
ins	2.5	3.0	4.2	5.0	3.9	2.5	1.6	1.5	2.3	6.4	6.8	3.9	**43.6**
Average sunshine per day													
hrs	6	5	4	3	3	4	4	4	4	3	4	5	**4**

JULY	AUGUST	SEPTEMBER	OCTOBER	NOVEMBER	DECEMBER

Europe

June is thought of as one of the nicest months for weather throughout Europe. It is not hot enough to be uncomfortable in the east, and it is one of the drier months in the west. The days are also long, and the sky sunnier than usual.

Europe is the most northerly of the densely inhabited parts of the world. The North Cape is 72°N and has continuous daylight for over two months. This is why Norway is called "the land of the midnight sun." The sight of the midnight sun attracts many people to make the long journey to the tip of Norway, but even places much farther south, such as northern Scotland, have only a brief night.

The sun is now as far north as it will go. The sun is never directly overhead in Europe, but it has now moved over North Africa, and many southern parts of Europe see a sun

▼ This map shows the highest temperatures expected during June. Use it to imagine what conditions are like in the early afternoon.

The effect of the North Atlantic Drift current has now ended, and daytime temperatures are becoming slightly higher in eastern Europe, where the effect of the ocean is least. They are still being held down all along the Norwegian coast, where cool winds continue to blow onshore. The south is the hottest part of the continent because the midday sun is highest in the sky there, and there is less cloud than further north. (The average temperatures for Europe in June, which include the effect of cold nights, are shown on the map on page 22.)

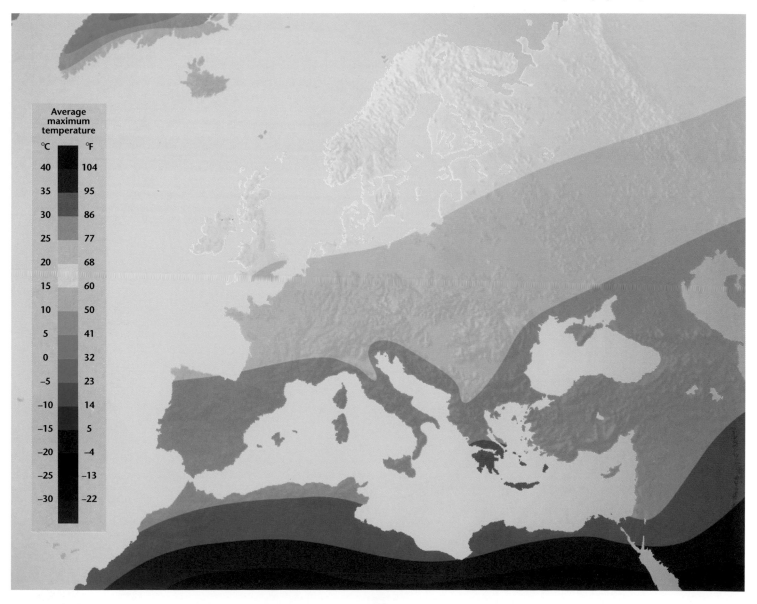

Average maximum temperature

°C	°F
40	104
35	95
30	86
25	77
20	68
15	60
10	50
5	41
0	32
−5	23
−10	14
−15	5
−20	−4
−25	−13
−30	−22

that is very high in the sky. The cool Mediterranean Sea water also make air sink, and this prevents cloud. As a result, countries that border the Mediterranean soak up the sun and by June are very hot. Athens, Greece, for example, can expect daytime highs of about 30°C/86°F and nighttime lows that go no lower than a warm 20°C/68°F.

In the Atlantic the main high-pressure system, called the Azores high, is off the western end of the Mediterranean, not only blocking moist air from the Mediterranean Sea, but also sending out ridges of high pressure northward. In June a ridge of high pressure often forms over the British Isles. It is called a "blocking high," and it deflects all the lows carried on the westerly winds over Iceland, far to the north. With fewer bands of cloud and rain, June can be a sunny month in the whole of northwestern Europe and even a month of drought.

▶ This is a picture taken at midnight from the North Cape of Norway on Midsummer's Day. The sun does not set for many weeks at this high latitude, but the changeable weather reduces the chances of seeing the sun at midnight without a covering of cloud!

▼ By June all of the trees have grown new leaves but still look fresh and green. The moisture held in the soil from the winter, coupled with warmer weather, allows upland grass, such as here in the highlands of Scotland, to grow rapidly. But the combination of moist air and higher temperatures also triggers thunderstorms, as can be seen in the background of this picture.

Central and Eastern Europe are not cooled by the North Atlantic Drift, and heat from the sun is soaking into the ground. Farther east the effect is even more dramatic, so that an intense low extends across from Europe through northern Asia. This low draws in air from the south and the west. In Europe the Alps tend to prevent air from moving north, and so most air comes off the Atlantic Ocean. Thus the natural flow of the westerly winds is reinforced by the continental low. The result is that moist air is sucked right across the continent and eastward into Asia.

The moist air and warm ground start to change the pattern of rain across the continent. Many places in the interior of Europe get more rain in summer than in winter. Most of this rain is in the form of thunder showers, and in June the ground is hot enough to set them off in abundance. As a result, the rainiest places are well inland, from France and Germany in the west, across the Hungarian Plain and toward Poland, through Moscow and across toward the steppes on the southeastern edges of the continent.

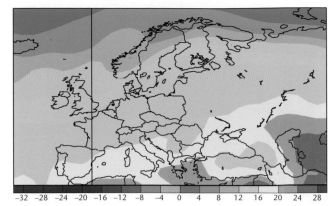

-32 -28 -24 -20 -16 -12 -8 -4 0 4 8 12 16 20 24 28

▲ This map shows the average air temperature over Europe (°C) in June.

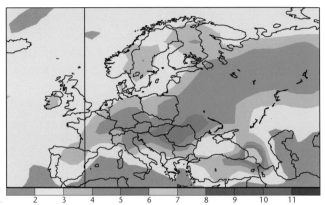

2 3 4 5 6 7 8 9 10 11

▲ This map shows the average amount of precipitation that falls over Europe (in mm/day) in June.

▼ This map shows the main weather systems and ocean currents in June.

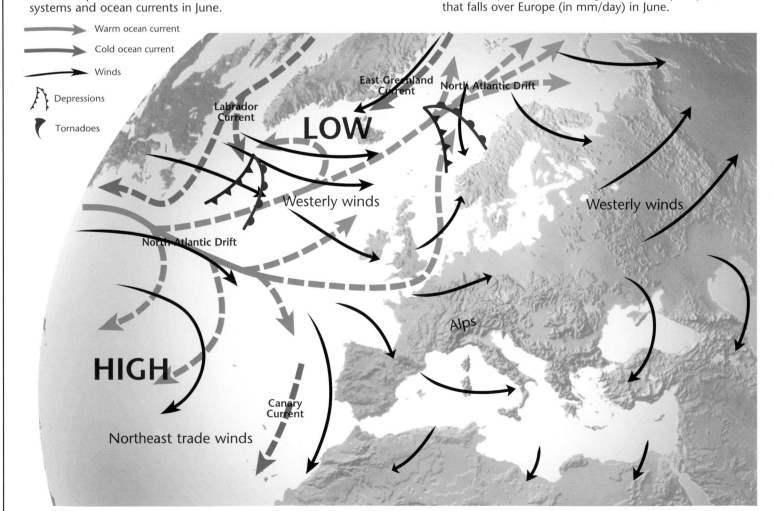

Warm ocean current
Cold ocean current
Winds
Depressions
Tornadoes

East Greenland Current
North Atlantic Drift
Labrador Current
LOW
Westerly winds
North Atlantic Drift
Westerly winds
Alps
HIGH
Canary Current
Northeast trade winds

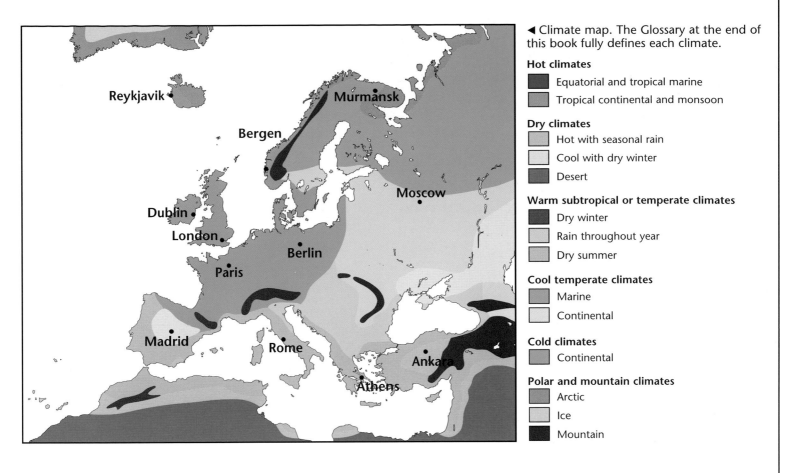

◄ Climate map. The Glossary at the end of this book fully defines each climate.

Hot climates
- Equatorial and tropical marine
- Tropical continental and monsoon

Dry climates
- Hot with seasonal rain
- Cool with dry winter
- Desert

Warm subtropical or temperate climates
- Dry winter
- Rain throughout year
- Dry summer

Cool temperate climates
- Marine
- Continental

Cold climates
- Continental

Polar and mountain climates
- Arctic
- Ice
- Mountain

Ankara

Daytime max. about 26°C/79°F, nighttime min. about 12°C/54°F

20°C | 68°F   37mm

1.5in

Athens

Daytime max. about 30°C/86°F, nighttime min. about 20°C/68°F

25°C | 77°F   7.4mm

0.3in

Bergen

Daytime max. about 16°C/61°F, nighttime min. about 10°C/50°F

13°C | 55°F   126mm

5.0in

Berlin

Daytime max. about 22°C/72°F, nighttime min. about 12°C/54°F

17°C | 63°F   76mm

3.0in

Dublin

Daytime max. about 18°C/64°F, nighttime min. about 9°C/48°F

14°C | 57°F   55mm

2.2in

London

Daytime max. about 20°C/68°F, nighttime min. about 12°C/54°F

16°C | 61°F   46mm

1.8in

Madrid

Daytime max. about 27°C/81°F, nighttime min. about 15°C/60°F

21°C | 70°F   31mm

1.2in

Moscow

Daytime max. about 21°C/70°F, nighttime min. about 11°C/52°F

16°C | 61°F   66mm

2.6in

Murmansk

Daytime max. about 17°C/63°F, nighttime min. about 6°C/43°F

9°C | 48°F   47mm

1.9in

Paris

Daytime max. about 23°C/73°F, nighttime min. about 13°C/55°F

17°C | 63°F   57mm

2.2in

Reykjavik

Daytime max. about 12°C/54°F, nighttime min. about 7°C/45°F

9°C | 48°F   45mm

1.8in

Rome
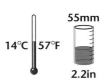

Daytime max. about 28°C/82°F, nighttime min. about 17°C/63°F

22°C | 72°F   34mm

1.3in

See the Quick reference on page 2 for an explanation of the symbols used here.

Berlin

Berlin lies in the center of Europe, partly affected by the moderating effects of the westerly winds coming from the Atlantic Ocean, but also influenced by the great cold Siberian high in winter and the heating up of the land in summer. This combination produces a more or less even pattern of precipitation through the year, but a hot, thundery summer with a rainfall maximum in June and a cold winter.

STATION: Berlin, Germany, is located at about 52.47°N 13.40°E. Height about 50m/164ft above sea level.

CLIMATE: Cool temperate, western margin, climate.

Berlin sits in the center of the low-lying part of northern Europe called the North European Plain. There are no mountain ranges to block the flow of westerly winds to Berlin, and so annual rainfall is quite heavy.

In summer the European continent heats up, and a low forms. Moist air flowing into the continent, combined with summer heating, mean that afternoon thunderstorms are common.

Berlin's rainfall peaks in summer, with nearly three-quarters of it falling between noon and 8 p.m. The rain is heavy but comes in short, sharp showers. Rain falls in Berlin on only two-thirds of the days that it falls in London, England, for example, so that summer days are much sunnier in Berlin than in London.

In winter the Siberian high pushes cold air across Europe. Berlin lies near the western edge of this air along a kind of battleground zone between cold air pushing west and warmer air carried by the westerly winds trying to push east. The cold high blocks the westward movement of lows for weeks on end. As a result, there is less precipitation in winter than in

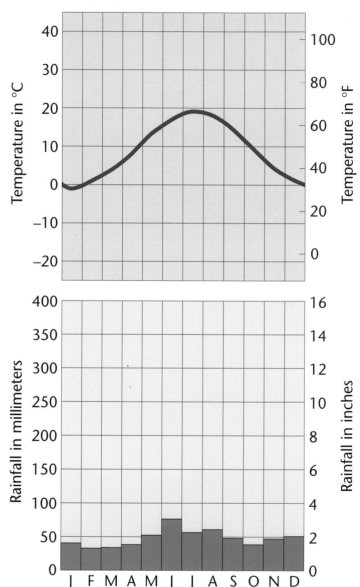

JANUARY **FEBRUARY** **MARCH** **APRIL** **MAY** **JUNE**

summer. The cold ground that develops under clear winter skies cools the air as it flows east over the continent, so that winter precipitation is almost entirely snow. Berlin has an average of 34 snow days, while London to the west only rarely experiences the cold Siberian air and has barely 5 snowy days in a year.

The winter high also produces calm weather and sinking air. Under these conditions there is little chance of pollution escaping from the city. Berlin is notorious for high pollution levels in winter. Cold air also often causes any moisture to condense and produce either low cloud or fog. This condition, known to meteorologists as "anticyclonic gloom," can last for days or weeks on end in the coldest part of a Berlin winter and produce raw, quite miserable conditions.

The change between winter and summer weather occurs when the cold winter high is replaced by a summer low. As a result, the change between summer and winter is quite abrupt, and spring and autumn are brief seasons.

The main problems farmers near Berlin face from the weather are late and early killing frosts, a drought in the growing season, or heavy crop-damaging rain at harvest time.

▲ Berlin center, near the Kurfurstendam, is a place of considerable sunshine in summer.

	Jan	Feb	Mar	Apr	May	Jun	Jul	Aug	Sep	Oct	Nov	Dec	Year
Average daily temperature													
°C	–1	1	4	8	14	17	19	18	14	9	4	1	**9**
°F	30	34	39	46	57	63	66	64	57	48	39	34	**48**
Average rainfall per month													
mm	42	33	34	39	53	76	57	60	48	39	47	51	**581**
ins	1.7	1.3	1.4	1.6	2.1	3.0	2.3	2.4	1.9	1.5	1.8	2.0	**22.9**
Average sunshine per day													
hrs	2	2	5	6	8	8	8	7	6	4	2	1	**5**

JULY	AUGUST	SEPTEMBER	OCTOBER	NOVEMBER	DECEMBER

Oceania and Hawaii

The southern half of Australia and all of New Zealand experience winter during June. The westerly winds have spread up from the Southern Ocean, bringing unsettled weather. By contrast, the tropical Pacific islands and northern Australia see trade winds and sunnier, drier weather.

The weather for much of this region is dominated by the subtropical high-pressure systems that lie in the Indian and Pacific oceans. In June they are near their most northerly positions, and this allows the westerly winds that circle the Southern Ocean to flow over much of the southern half of Australia and over all of New Zealand.

As the westerly winds pass, they carry depressions containing bands of cloud and rain. The depressions bring together warm air from the tropics and cold air from the Antarctic. Areas affected by depressions therefore get hot

▼ This map shows the highest temperatures expected during June. Use it to imagine what conditions are like in the early afternoon.

There is a large contrast between the heat of the tropical islands, which are surrounded by warm ocean waters, and the coolness of much of Australia and New Zealand. In Australia it is not uncommon for large areas west of the Snowy Mountains to have daily temperatures below 10°C/50°F, and on the mountains themselves conditions are below freezing every day, so that skiing is a common pastime. (The average temperatures for Oceania and Hawaii in June, which include the effect of cold nights, are shown on the map on page 28.)

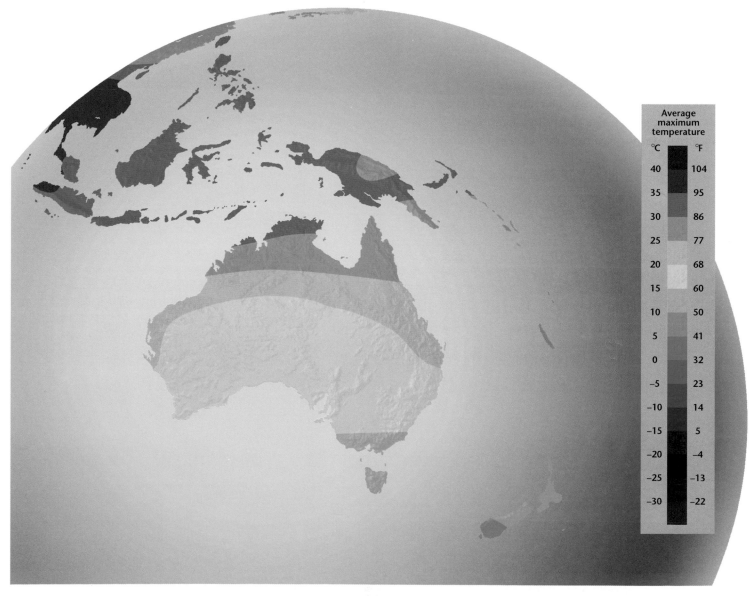

Average maximum temperature	
°C	°F
40	104
35	95
30	86
25	77
20	68
15	60
10	50
5	41
0	32
−5	23
−10	14
−15	5
−20	−4
−25	−13
−30	−22

muggy conditions while the tropical air passes overhead and then a sudden change to cold as Antarctic air is pulled north in the wake of the depression. The frontal zone between the two types of air is often marked by a long line of heavy, thundery rainstorms.

Depressions make June a month of considerable rainfall in many parts of southern Australia. For example, Perth receives an average of 182mm/7.2in, Sydney 129mm/5.1in, and Adelaide 70mm/2.7in.

In New Zealand the westerly winds stretch as far north as Auckland, on the North Island. It is a city more used to the warmer effects of the trade winds. People therefore notice the weather getting cold, and after a warm summer the inevitability of rain makes everyone feel gloomy. And, as in other parts of New Zealand and southern Australia, it is unusual for people to have central heating in their homes because it is needed for such a short period in the year. Even in Auckland frost can occur in June, so those without central heating feel cold.

▲ Snow dusts eucalyptus forests as it reaches lower down the slopes of the Australian Alps in the south of the Great Dividing Range. The ski season officially starts in the first week in June, though it is normally at its best in July, August, and September.

The Southern Alps and volcanic mountains in New Zealand also start their ski season this month.

▼ Trade wind clouds over the Great Barrier Reef. Australians from the sun-starved south travel north to soak up the warmth as the far north approaches its driest time of year.

By contrast, the tropical north of Australia is experiencing its dry season, with sunny skies and only very occasional rainshowers. This is because the overhead sun is so far to the north that the equatorial low pressure (that causes the rainy season) is far into the northern hemisphere. Northern Australia is now in the path of southeast trade winds, which, as they blow across the continent, lose most of their moisture. In Darwin these winds are now offshore, dry winds. In Port Moresby, Papua New Guinea, some rain still falls because the trade winds blow onshore, and the air has picked up some moisture between Australia and Papua New Guinea as it passes over the Torres Strait.

June is also a drier month for many of the tropical Pacific islands. Although they get rainfall throughout the year, in June the trade winds blow closer to the equator, and the subtropical highs are nearer, so the chances of rain are lower.

This is also the month with the lowest rainfall in Hawaii. In this case it is because the subtropical high pressure in the Pacific has moved north, and so the winds die down. Because the rainfall in Hawaii is mainly from trade winds, when these winds blow less strongly, there is less rain.

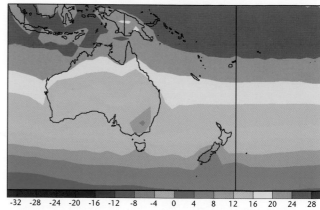

-32 -28 -24 -20 -16 -12 -8 -4 0 4 8 12 16 20 24 28

▲ This map shows the average air temperature over Oceania and Hawaii (°C) in June.

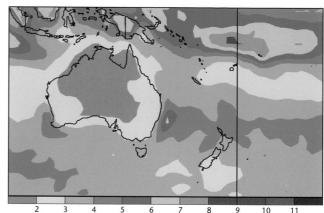

2 3 4 5 6 7 8 9 10 11

▲ This map shows the average amount of precipitation that falls over Oceania and Hawaii (in mm/day) in June.

▼ This map shows the main weather systems and ocean currents in June.

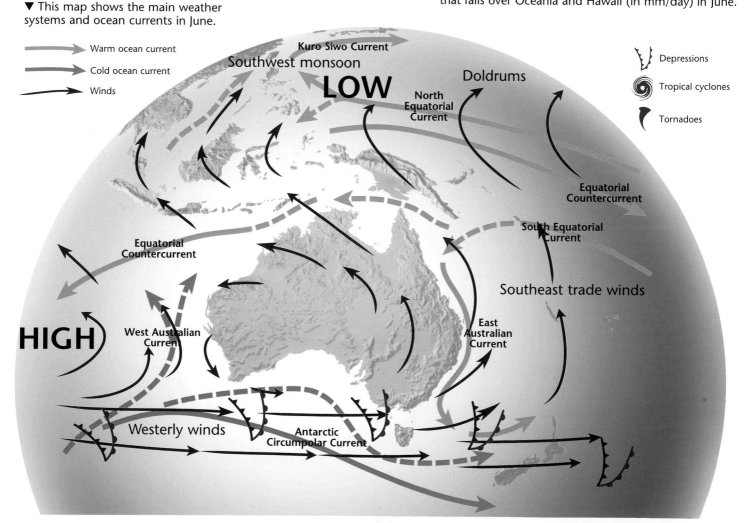

Warm ocean current

Cold ocean current

Winds

Kuro Siwo Current

Southwest monsoon

Doldrums

LOW

North Equatorial Current

Depressions

Tropical cyclones

Tornadoes

Equatorial Countercurrent

Equatorial Countercurrent

South Equatorial Current

HIGH

West Australian Current

Southeast trade winds

East Australian Current

Westerly winds

Antarctic Circumpolar Current

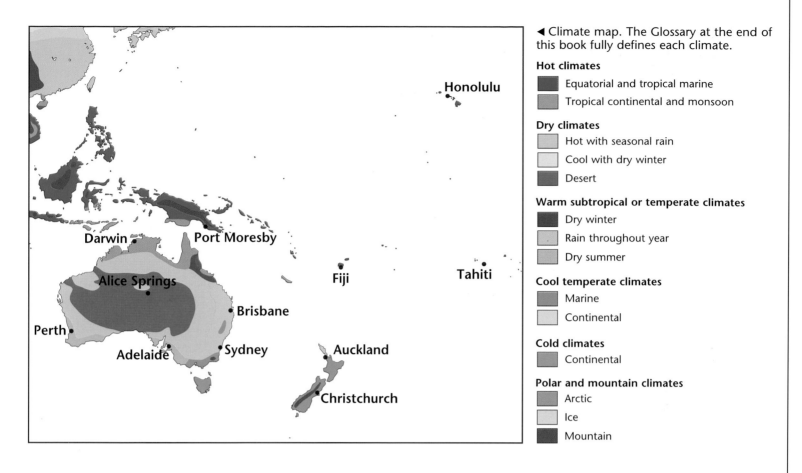

◀ Climate map. The Glossary at the end of this book fully defines each climate.

Hot climates
- Equatorial and tropical marine
- Tropical continental and monsoon

Dry climates
- Hot with seasonal rain
- Cool with dry winter
- Desert

Warm subtropical or temperate climates
- Dry winter
- Rain throughout year
- Dry summer

Cool temperate climates
- Marine
- Continental

Cold climates
- Continental

Polar and mountain climates
- Arctic
- Ice
- Mountain

Adelaide
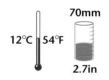

Daytime max. about 16°C/61°F, nighttime min. about 8°C/46°F

 12°C 54°F — 70mm / 2.7in

Alice Springs

Daytime max. about 19°C/66°F, nighttime min. about 5°C/41°F

 12°C 54°F — 17mm / 0.7in

Auckland
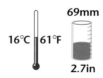

Daytime max. about 14°C/57°F, nighttime min. about 9°C/48°F

 12°C 54°F — 126mm / 4.9in

Brisbane

Daytime max. about 21°C/70°F, nighttime min. about 11°C/52°F

 16°C 61°F — 69mm / 2.7in

Christchurch

Daytime max. about 11°C/52°F, nighttime min. about 2°C/36°F

 6°C 43°F — 65mm / 2.6in

Darwin

Daytime max. about 31°C/88°F, nighttime min. about 21°C/70°F

 26°C 79°F — 3mm / 0.1in

Fiji

Daytime max. about 27°C/81°F, nighttime min. about 21°C/70°F

 23°C 73°F — 141mm / 5.6in

Honolulu

Daytime max. about 27°C/81°F, nighttime min. about 22°C/72°F

 26°C 79°F — 9.7mm / 0.4in

Perth

Daytime max. about 18°C/64°F, nighttime min. about 10°C/50°F

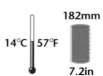 14°C 57°F — 182mm / 7.2in

Port Moresby

Daytime max. about 29°C/84°F, nighttime min. about 23°C/73°F

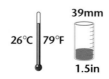 26°C 79°F — 39mm / 1.5in

Sydney

Daytime max. about 16°C/61°F, nighttime min. about 9°C/48°F

 13°C 55°F — 129mm / 5.1in

Tahiti

Daytime max. about 30°C/86°F, nighttime min. about 21°C/70°F

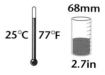 25°C 77°F — 68mm / 2.7in

See the Quick reference on page 2 for an explanation of the symbols used here.

Brisbane

Brisbane lies at the junction between the tropics, with a monsoon season, and the midlatitudes, with a cool winter. June marks the beginning of the driest part of the year.

STATION: Brisbane, Australia, is located at about 27.50°S 153.00°E. Height about 38m/124ft above sea level.

CLIMATE: Warm temperate, eastern margin climate.

Brisbane lies near the boundary between the tropical climate of northern Queensland, with its monsoon rains, and the warm temperate climate of New South Wales, with its summer and autumn rains and cooler, drier winter and spring.

In Brisbane there is a seasonal reversal of winds like that found in the tropics, but there are no clearly marked wet and dry seasons.

So, for example, in July, which is the height of the dry season for northern Queensland, some rain falls in Brisbane due to the onshore movement of moisture-bearing trade winds. Rainfall is, however, in the form of short, sharp showers, with long sunny periods in between. In fact, at this time of year the sunnier skies also allow the occasional touch of frost on the high ground away from the coast.

From October, as the overhead midday sun moves into the southern hemisphere, the continent heats up, and a low-pressure center develops over the northern part of Australia. This is the time when rain-bearing (monsoon) winds begin to blow, and the wet season begins, reaching its height in Brisbane during December, January, and February.

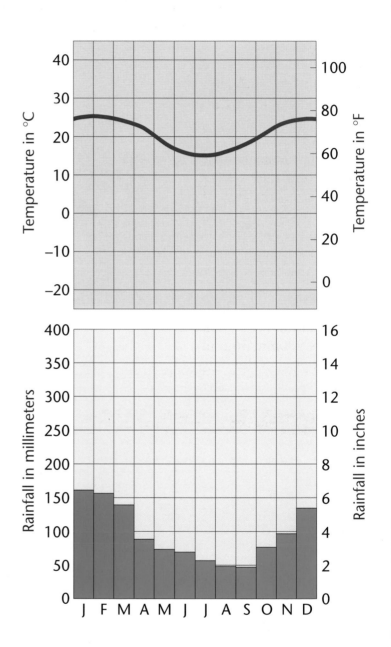

JANUARY	FEBRUARY	MARCH	APRIL	MAY	JUNE

The rain is not as continuous as it is farther north, and there are many dry days. The heavy, thundery rain occurs whenever slow-moving rainstorms move southeast, steered by northwesterly winds high in the atmosphere. Occasionally these storms have tornadoes associated with them.

Brisbane is also one of the Australian cities most vulnerable to tropical cyclones. Such storms are an essentially equatorial feature that originate in the Solomon Islands and travel southwest, swinging first south and then southeast before they reach the coast. On most occasions the tropical cyclones follow a track that remains offshore, so that only their outer fringes affect the city. The result is high winds and heavy downpours, but no more. However, sometimes they track across the coast, and then they can do considerable damage. They also bring torrential rain, sometimes as much as 900mm/36in in a day. Tropical cyclones can

affect the whole of the Queensland coast between December and April, but January to March are the most common months for tropical cyclones to come onshore.

At this time of year the temperatures are high, and there is always considerable moisture in the air, so a combination of heat and high humidity make the weather oppressively muggy.

▲ The remains of a tropical storm linger in the sky over Brisbane.

	Jan	Feb	Mar	Apr	May	Jun	Jul	Aug	Sep	Oct	Nov	Dec	Year
Average daily temperature													
°C	25	25	24	22	18	16	15	16	18	21	24	24	**21**
°F	77	77	75	72	64	61	60	61	64	70	75	75	**70**
Average rainfall per month													
mm	161	157	140	89	73	69	57	48	47	77	97	134	**1,151**
ins	6.3	6.2	5.5	3.5	2.9	2.7	2.2	1.8	1.8	3.0	3.8	5.3	**45.3**
Average sunshine per day													
hrs	8	7	7	7	7	7	7	8	8	8	8	9	**8**

JULY	AUGUST	SEPTEMBER	OCTOBER	NOVEMBER	DECEMBER

Asia

June sees the start of the Indian monsoon, one of the world's most extraordinary weather events. In fact, rain falls over much of the continent this month, which, coupled with high temperature, makes conditions unpleasantly muggy.

By June the heat from the sun is producing two vast areas of low pressure across Asia separated by the Himalaya Mountains and the Tibetan plateau.

As eastern Asia "breathes in," it draws moist, warm air off the western Pacific and brings the rainy season – the monsoon. The area affected by torrential monsoon rain has been spreading steadily northward for a month now, and in June it affects Southeast Asia, the Philippines, and at the end of the month China.

Northern Asia has also begun to warm up, completely removing the cold winter high and letting air flood in from the south and the west. This is the time of year when the

▼ This map shows the highest temperatures expected during June. Use it to imagine what conditions are like in the early afternoon.

Notice how hot it is over northern India and Pakistan. At this time of year there is no cloud to cut out the heat from the sun, and so the land gets hotter and hotter. By contrast, it is cooler in eastern Asia, for here rain is falling.

Less dramatic, but very important, is the heat that builds up in the steppes of Central Asia between the plateau of Tibet and Siberia. This warm corridor is used by westerly winds to bring rain to the steppes. (The average temperatures for Asia in June, which include the effect of cold nights, are shown on the map on page 34.)

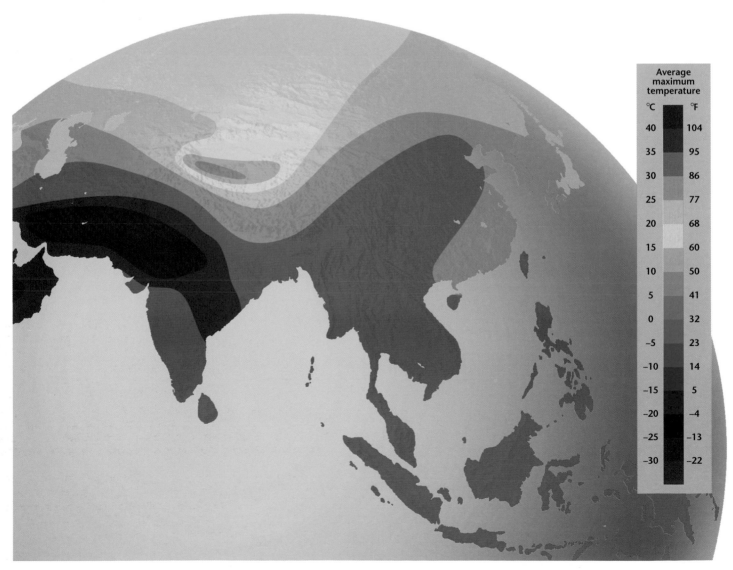

Average maximum temperature	
°C	°F
40	104
35	95
30	86
25	77
20	68
15	60
10	50
5	41
0	32
−5	23
−10	14
−15	5
−20	−4
−25	−13
−30	−22

westerly winds can reach right across the continent. Although the amount of rain they bring is not large, it is vital for the grass and the crops of these naturally parched steppe lands.

The deepest low stretches from Arabia across to India. But although air flows across the Indian Ocean toward this low, no rain falls, and the land remains dry, dusty, and increasingly humid and uncomfortable. The rainfall map on page 34 shows this clearly: over the Indian Ocean torrential rain is falling just off the coast, a tantalizing distance away, but over India and Pakistan there is hardly any.

So, June sees one of the most remarkable of all weather events play out on the Indian subcontinent. During this month the Indian monsoon breaks, meaning that the rains, so long delayed compared with other areas of tropical Asia, begin.

The reason for the strange nature of the Indian subcontinent is the presence of the great range of the Himalayas to the north. They act like a wall, stopping this part of Asia from "breathing in." Instead, a wind high in the air (called the subtropical jet stream) continually pumps air into the sky over India. This explains why winds continue to blow offshore.

It is not until the end of June that the jet stream finally veers north of the Himalayas and stops pumping its air across India. Relieved of this air pressure, India suddenly "breathes in" like the

▲ Monsoon clouds gather over the mountains of Malaysia.

◄ In Southeast Asia the monsoon is well under way, the sky is overcast, and the air hot and humid. Traditional village houses are built on stilts to allow the rainwater to wash under them during the wet season.

rest of Asia, bringing a sudden rush of moist air from the Indian Ocean. It doesn't show up on the monthly statistics because they span the dry start of the month and the incredibly wet end of the month. But to be in India at this time is to experience a sudden deluge from the sky and to see people rush out of their houses and dance, soaking wet, in the streets. Although they know that the streets will soon be awash with water, at least the monsoon has now broken, and they can experience cooler, less ferociously hot weather.

June is also the month when, along with May, the chances of a tropical cyclone striking the Bay of Bengal or the Arabian Sea are at their highest. With tropical cyclones and monsoons combined, this is a month that can spell horrific disaster, especially to low-lying and vulnerable places like Bangladesh, where floods in the rivers and tidal waves from the tropical cyclone can combine to put a third of the country under water.

| -32 | -28 | -24 | -20 | -16 | -12 | -8 | -4 | 0 | 4 | 8 | 12 | 16 | 20 | 24 | 28 |

▲ This map shows the average air temperature over Asia (°C) in June.

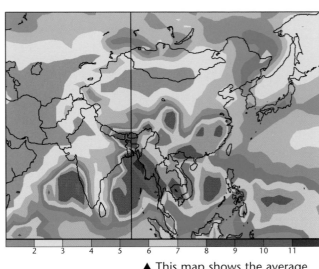

| 2 | 3 | 4 | 5 | 6 | 7 | 8 | 9 | 10 | 11 |

▲ This map shows the average amount of precipitation that falls over Asia (in mm/day) in June.

▼ This map shows the main weather systems and ocean currents in June.

⟶ Warm ocean current

⟶ Cold ocean current

⟶ Winds

Depressions

Tropical cyclones

Tornadoes

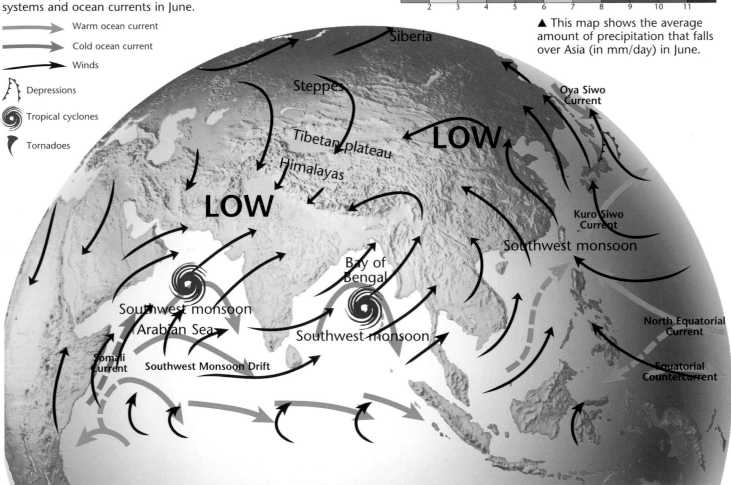

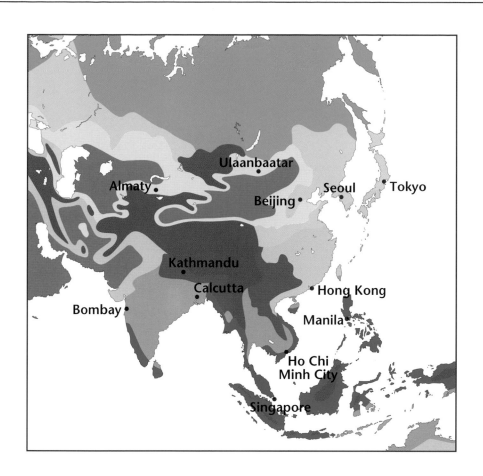

◀ Climate map. The Glossary at the end of this book fully defines each climate.

Hot climates
- Equatorial and tropical marine
- Tropical continental and monsoon

Dry climates
- Hot with seasonal rain
- Cool with dry winter
- Desert

Warm subtropical or temperate climates
- Dry winter
- Rain throughout year
- Dry summer

Cool temperate climates
- Marine
- Continental

Cold climates
- Continental

Polar and mountain climates
- Arctic
- Ice
- Mountain

Almaty

Daytime max. about 20°C/68°F, nighttime min. about 10°C/50°F

20°C | 68°F — 57mm / 2.2in

Beijing

Daytime max. about 31°C/88°F, nighttime min. about 18°C/64°F

24°C | 75°F — 78mm / 3.1in

Bombay
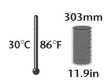

Daytime max. about 32°C/90°F, nighttime min. about 26°C/79°F

29°C | 84°F — 518mm / 20.4in

Calcutta
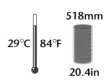

Daytime max. about 33°C/91°F, nighttime min. about 26°C/79°F

30°C | 86°F — 303mm / 11.9in

Ho Chi Minh City

Daytime max. about 32°C/90°F, nighttime min. about 24°C/75°F

309mm
27°C | 81°F — 309mm / 12.2in

Hong Kong

Daytime max. about 29°C/84°F, nighttime min. about 26°C/79°F

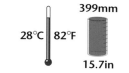
28°C | 82°F — 399mm / 15.7in

Kathmandu

Daytime max. about 29°C/84°F, nighttime min. about 19°C/66°F

24°C | 75°F — 201mm / 7.9in

Manila

Daytime max. about 33°C/91°F, nighttime min. about 24°C/75°F

28°C | 82°F — 262mm / 10.3in

Seoul

Daytime max. about 27°C/81°F, nighttime min. about 16°C/61°F

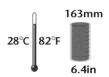
20°C | 68°F — 116mm / 4.6in

Singapore

Daytime max. about 31°C/88°F, nighttime min. about 24°C/75°F

28°C | 82°F — 163mm / 6.4in

Tokyo

Daytime max. about 24°C/75°F, nighttime min. about 17°C/63°F

176mm
21°C | 70°F — 176mm / 6.9in

Ulaanbaatar
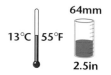

Daytime max. about 21°C/70°F, nighttime min. about 7°C/45°F

64mm
13°C | 55°F — 64mm / 2.5in

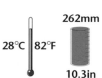
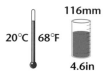

See the Quick reference on page 2 for an explanation of the symbols used here.

Tokyo

Although it is on an island, the main influence on the climate of Tokyo is the large continent of Asia. During winter, when cold air blows from China, Tokyo experiences cold, sometimes snowy winters. By contrast, in June it is hot and thundery, and by late summer there are some effects from the monsoon.

STATION: Tokyo, Japan, is located at about 35.68°N 139.69°E. Height about 5m/16ft above sea level.

CLIMATE: Cool temperate, eastern margin climate.

Japan occupies a curved chain of mountainous volcanic islands off the coast of eastern Asia. Because Japan stretches through a wide range of latitudes, conditions in the north (which is 45°N) and the south (which is 32°N) are very different. Tokyo is about halfway between these two extremes. Tokyo lies at about the same latitude as Norfolk, Virginia, and the island of Gibraltar in the Mediterranean Sea.

Japan is surrounded by water and so does not have quite such hot summers or very cold winters as many places on the nearby Chinese mainland. In a similar way the seas allow the air to pick up moisture and ensure that rainfall is more even through the year, without the dry season that is typical of winter in China.

One of the important influences on Japan's weather is the warm ocean current called the Kuro Siwo that washes the country's eastern shores. It is equivalent to the Gulf Stream in the Atlantic Ocean off the East Coast of North America.

Tokyo, being halfway along the coast, is where the cold ocean current flowing down from the north (the Oya Siwo) meets the warm current (Kuro Siwo) moving up from the tropics. And

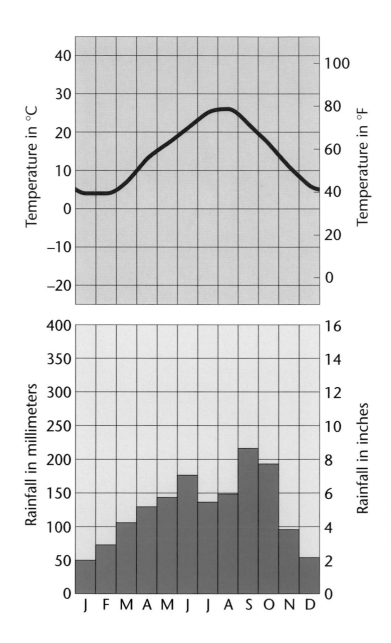

JANUARY **FEBRUARY** **MARCH** **APRIL** **MAY** **JUNE**

just as the cold Labrador Current hugs the coast of North America and pushes the Gulf Stream off across the ocean, so the cold Oya Siwo Current flows southward along the coast between China and Japan, forcing the warm Kuro Siwo to flow off the eastern side of Japan.

As a result, Japan, like northeastern North America, does not get much benefit from the warmth of the ocean current. However, the warm water does provide a focus for storm tracks. As a result, depressions, with their bands of cloud and rain, are a winter feature. This is why the Japanese climate is much more variable than the nearby continental climate.

The other big influence on the climate of Japan is the Asian monsoon. During the winter, when the Asian continent develops a high-pressure area, and the continent "breathes out," the monsoon wind is northwesterly, bringing much rain and snow to the western sides of the islands, and leaving the eastern (rainshadow) side (including Tokyo) comparatively dry. Thus Tokyo has only 218mm/8.7in of rain in the three winter months, while on the west coast 800mm/32in of rain falls. These moist, cold winds feel raw on the west coast, while the east is sheltered, and drier so Tokyo feels more pleasant.

In spring the high over Asia changes into a low, and the continent "breathes in." Spring is short, but it brings sunnier weather for a while. It is often regarded as the most pleasant time of the year. It is also the time when blossom bursts out on all of the trees. By summer the monsoon winds reverse, and the east coast becomes wetter and the west coast drier. West coast locations actually have more rain in winter than summer, while east coast cities like Tokyo have the reverse. Two-thirds of Tokyo's rain falls in the three summer months, and with it come cloudy skies and only limited sunshine.

The late spring and early summer rains peak in May and June. They are called the Plum Rains, or *Bai-U*. July and August are a bit drier; then there is a renewed rainfall in September and October, much of it connected to the passage of typhoons that spread up the China Sea from the Philippines.

	Jan	Feb	Mar	Apr	May	Jun	Jul	Aug	Sep	Oct	Nov	Dec	Year
Average daily temperature													
°C	4	4	7	13	17	21	25	26	22	17	11	6	**15**
°F	39	39	45	55	63	70	77	79	72	63	52	43	**60**
Average rainfall per month													
mm	50	72	106	129	144	176	136	149	216	194	96	54	**1,523**
ins	2.0	2.8	4.2	5.1	5.7	6.9	5.3	5.8	8.5	7.6	3.8	2.1	**60.0**
Average sunshine per day													
hrs	6	6	6	7	6	5	6	7	5	4	5	5	**6**

JULY	AUGUST	SEPTEMBER	OCTOBER	NOVEMBER	DECEMBER

Africa and the Middle East

June is one of the driest months in Africa. In the southern hemisphere it is the dry season, while in the north fearsomely hot, dry conditions extend from the Sahara Desert and Arabia to the shores of the Mediterranean Sea. Only places close to the equator have rain.

The overhead midday sun is now at the Tropic of Cancer (22.5°N), which extends right across the Sahara Desert. Each day the sun beats down on the Sahara Desert, bringing average temperatures to over 30°C/86°F and daytime maximums to 43°C/109°F in Timbuktu and 42°C/108°F in Riyadh.

You might expect this vast area of baking-hot ground to heat the air above it so much that it would rise, forming a low that would suck in air from all around. But this does not happen because the Sahara is at a latitude where air sinks worldwide. The sinking effect completely overwhelms attempts by the hot air to rise and holds it quite close to the ground, so that the air gets even hotter.

▼ This map shows the highest temperatures expected during June. Use it to imagine what conditions are like in the early afternoon.

The hottest place by far is the great band of North Africa and Arabia, which has temperatures above 40°C/104°F. Temperatures are lower over the equator because clouds block the sun for part of the day. Clouds are low too in East Africa because of the altitude of the land. The south is relatively cold because it is winter in the southern hemisphere. (The average temperatures for Africa in June, which include the effect of cold nights, are shown on the map on page 40.)

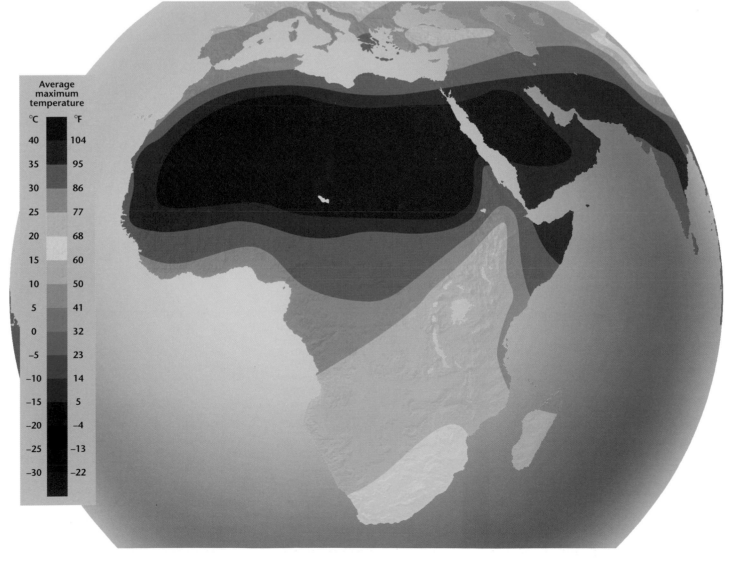

Average maximum temperature

°C	°F
40	104
35	95
30	86
25	77
20	68
15	60
10	50
5	41
0	32
−5	23
−10	14
−15	5
−20	−4
−25	−13
−30	−22

In fact, the effect of the sinking air is to make air from the Sahara flow toward the equator. However, when it reaches Mali and other countries of the Sahel (a transitional region between the Sahara Desert and the wetter savannas to the south), it meets the equatorial low, which in June is nearly at its northern limit. Here the hot, dry air rises over the hot, moist air pulled from the south and the Gulf of Guinea. This hot air has become very humid as it passed over the gulf. It typically produces huge thunderstorms.

The flow of air northward is the West African monsoon. In June and July it reaches the Sahel countries to give them their life-saving rain. But the position to which the rains reach varies each year. Some years the rains are plentiful in these countries; in other years they come late and finish early, releasing too little rain for the crops to grow. In such years famine is widespread.

On average, Timbuktu receives 19mm/0.7in in June, but this masks extreme variations from year to year.

The air being pulled over Africa from the Mediterranean is slightly cooled. It causes a permanent sea breeze at this time of the year, making the coastal regions much more bearable than places inland.

In the south it is the dry season, and in the extreme south, winter. A weak high develops over the southern part of the continent, connecting the subtropical highs in the oceans.

▼ To survive in the desert mountains of North Africa, good protection is needed from the heat and drying power of the wind. This traditional costume concentrates on protecting the head from the sun and, through loose clothing, making the body more comfortable.

Meanwhile, the goats get ever more desperate for food and ever more daring. These goats are expert tree-climbers.

▲ In the equatorial forests of Africa the intensity of the rains is making the rivers run high.

▼ The monsoon rains reach north of the grasslands to the countries of the Sahel just south of the Sahara Desert.

So, although winds are blowing onshore, they cannot rise, and no rain falls. Most of South Africa is relatively dry, with cool but sunny weather. The only exception is Cape Town. Here the westerly winds, with their bands of cloud and rain, just reach this, the most southerly part of Africa to produce changeable weather.

It is too hot for most people to visit the northern deserts, and so June is part of the low season for tourist destinations such as Cairo. In East Africa June is a dry month, and the coast of Kenya is a popular destination. The south coast of West Africa is hot and sultry, so few people go there. Although it is winter in South Africa, many people enjoy the cool, sunny, dry weather. Only the extreme south, with its Mediterranean winter, is off the tourist track.

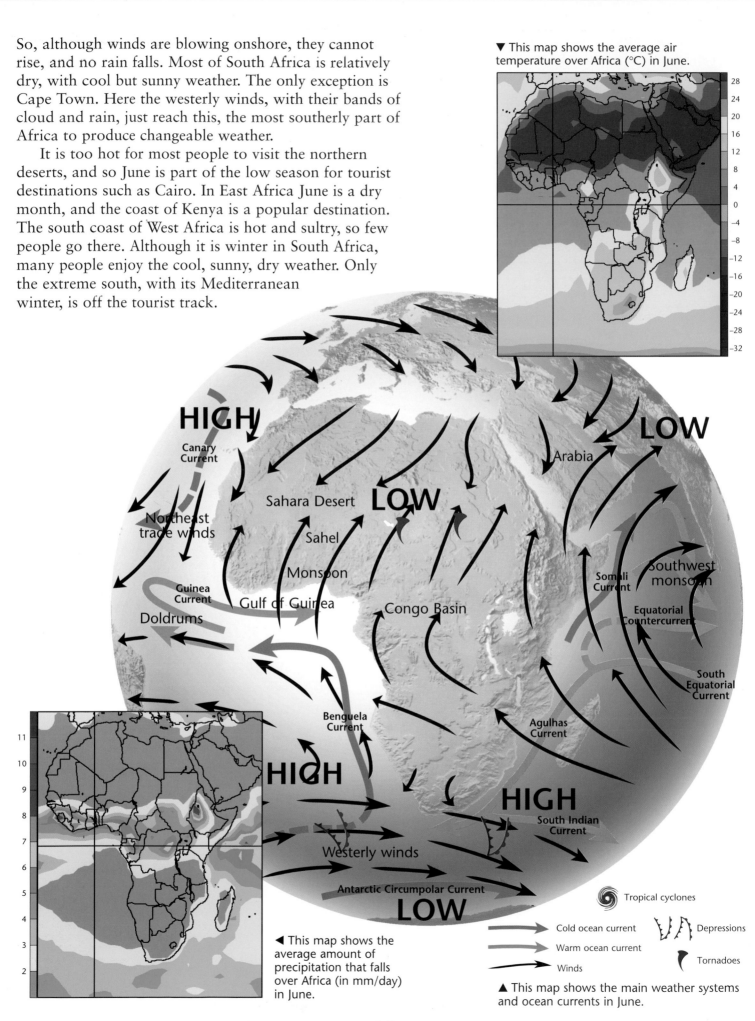

▼ This map shows the average air temperature over Africa (°C) in June.

◀ This map shows the average amount of precipitation that falls over Africa (in mm/day) in June.

▲ This map shows the main weather systems and ocean currents in June.

○ Tropical cyclones

→ Cold ocean current

→ Warm ocean current

→ Winds

∨∧ Depressions

▸ Tornadoes

40

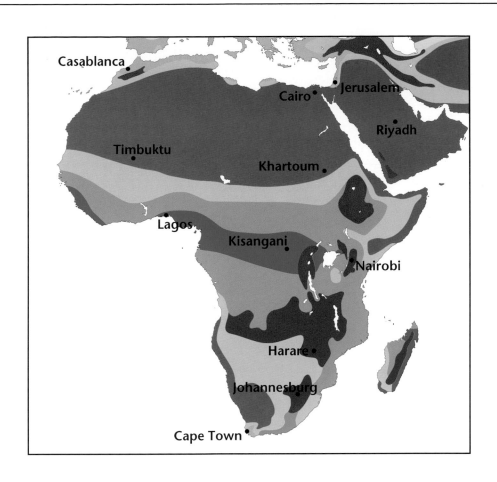

◄ Climate map. The Glossary at the end of this book fully defines each climate.

Hot climates
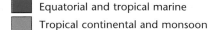 Equatorial and tropical marine
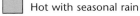 Tropical continental and monsoon

Dry climates
Hot with seasonal rain
Cool with dry winter
 Desert

Warm subtropical or temperate climates
Dry winter
 Rain throughout year
Dry summer

Cool temperate climates
Marine
Continental

Cold climates
Continental

Polar and mountain climates
Arctic
Ice
Mountain

Cairo

Daytime max. about 35°C/95°F, nighttime min. about 20°C/68°F

27°C | 81°F   0.2mm / 0.0in

Cape Town

Daytime max. about 18°C/64°F, nighttime min. about 8°C/46°F

13°C | 55°F   105mm / 4.1in

Casablanca

Daytime max. about 26°C/79°F, nighttime min. about 16°C/61°F

20°C | 68°F   5.7mm / 0.2in

Harare

Daytime max. about 21°C/70°F, nighttime min. about 7°C/45°F

14°C | 57°F   2.8mm / 0.1in

Jerusalem

Daytime max. about 29°C/84°F, nighttime min. about 16°C/61°F

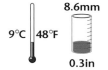
22°C | 72°F   0.0mm / 0.0in

Johannesburg

Daytime max. about 17°C/63°F, nighttime min. about 1°C/30°F

9°C | 48°F   8.6mm / 0.3in

Khartoum

Daytime max. about 41°C/106°F, nighttime min. about 26°C/79°F

34°C | 93°F   7.2mm / 0.3in

Kisangani

Daytime max. about 30°C/86°F, nighttime min. about 21°C/70°F

24°C | 75°F   128mm / 5.0in

Lagos

Daytime max. about 29°C/84°F, nighttime min. about 23°C/73°F

26°C | 79°F   414mm / 16.3in

Nairobi

Daytime max. about 21°C/70°F, nighttime min. about 12°C/54°F

16°C | 61°F   40mm / 1.6in

Riyadh

Daytime max. about 42°C/108°F, nighttime min. about 25°C/77°F

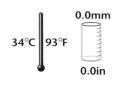
34°C | 93°F   0.0mm / 0.0in

Timbuktu

Daytime max. about 43°C/109°F, nighttime min. about 27°C/81°F

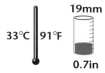
33°C | 91°F   19mm / 0.7in

See the Quick reference on page 2 for an explanation of the symbols used here.

Casablanca

Casablanca lies on the Atlantic coast of North Africa. With a cold offshore current, the summers are sunny but cooler than in the Mediterranean, and very different from the scorching Sahara Desert that is a short distance inland. Virtually no rain falls between June and September.

STATION: Casablanca, Morocco, is located at about 33.6°N 7.6°W. Height about 60m/200ft above sea level.

CLIMATE: Warm temperate, western margin (Mediterranean) climate.

Casablanca sits on the coast of northwest Africa. It faces the Atlantic Ocean. The weather there is dominated by the movement of the subtropical (Azores) high centered over the Atlantic Ocean and the cold ocean current that washes the shores.

Throughout the summer the Azores high is at its strongest and most northerly. Sitting almost directly off the Moroccan coast, the Azores high is a region of sinking air that prevents any cloud from forming. It creates the long, sunny, and cloudless summers that are so typical of a Mediterranean style of climate.

The weather is also greatly influenced by a cold coastal current (the Canaries Current) that flows offshore. The situation is very like that of coastal California or Perth, Australia. The cold ocean current cools the air flowing inland and holds down the temperatures at the coast, so that July temperatures in Casablanca are just 22°C/72°F, while in the Sahara Desert inland they may be over 40°C/105°F. This effect is a true sea breeze, with air being sucked onto the land by the hot Sahara Desert. The sea breeze makes the Moroccan coast unusually cool and pleasant compared with most of inland North

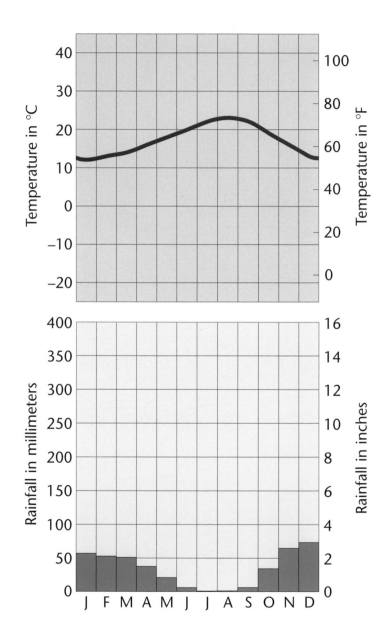

Africa and explains why it is a popular tourist destination.

In the winter the Azores high both weakens and slips slightly south, allowing westerly winds to carry depressions, with their bands of cloud and rain, through the Mediterranean.

As the depressions brush past the Moroccan shores, they first draw hot air off the Sahara Desert. These hot dry winds are often filled with dust. Then the depressions pull cold air from the northwest, bringing cool, cloudy weather with rain off the ocean. As a result, conditions in winter are very unsettled.

Because the rain is closely connected to the position of the Azores high, the rainfall in Casablanca is strongly seasonal, with almost none falling in the summer. The natural vegetation therefore does most of its growing in the winter rainy season, just as it does in California and Perth. This is because, even though the weather is cool, it is never cold enough to stop plants from growing. During winter, therefore, the whole north and northeast coast of Morocco become green. In contrast, when the summer drought begins, the plants die off, and the landscape looks brown and barren.

In Casablanca the coastal breeze blowing over a cold ocean current frequently produces low cloud and fog during the summertime, although nowhere near as much as in San Francisco.

▲▶ Casablanca's new and old towns.

	Jan	Feb	Mar	Apr	May	Jun	Jul	Aug	Sep	Oct	Nov	Dec	Year
Average daily temperature													
°C	12	13	14	16	18	20	22	23	22	19	16	13	**17**
°F	54	55	57	61	64	68	72	73	72	66	61	55	**63**
Average rainfall per month													
mm	57	53	51	38	21	5.7	0.3	0.7	6.1	34	65	73	**406**
ins	2.2	2.1	2.0	1.5	0.8	0.2	0.0	0.0	0.2	1.3	2.6	2.9	**16.0**
Average sunshine per day													
hrs	5	7	7	9	9	10	11	10	9	8	6	5	**8**

JULY	AUGUST	SEPTEMBER	OCTOBER	NOVEMBER	DECEMBER

Glossary

AIR PRESSURE: the force per square meter exerted by the air on the ground. It is caused by gravity pulling air molecules toward the center of the earth or by air flowing into a region faster than it flows out.

ALEUTIAN LOW: the low frequently found over the North Pacific, particularly in winter. Represents an area where depressions are frequent.

ANTICYCLONE: a region of sinking and outflowing air in which the winds move clockwise in the northern hemisphere and counterclockwise in the southern hemisphere. Anticyclones are regions of high-pressure air and so are often called simply highs. Anticyclones are associated with settled weather.

ANTICYCLONIC GLOOM: prolonged dull conditions produced by dense low cloud that is associated with anticyclones in winter. Common over midlatitude continental areas.

ARCTIC CLIMATE: a cold climate with a very brief warm season of less than three months above 6°C/43°F.

ASPECT: the direction in which a thing faces. Geographers particularly apply this term to the direction in which a slope is facing in relation to the sun, since this influences plant growth and where people choose to build.

ATMOSPHERE: the region of gases that surrounds the earth.

AZORES HIGH: the subtropical high usually positioned over the eastern side of the North Atlantic Ocean, level with North Africa but occasionally extending up to affect western areas of Europe. Stronger in summer than in winter.

BEAUFORT SCALE: A scale for measuring wind speed in units from force 0 (calm) to force 12 (hurricane force).

BLIZZARD: a combination of snow and strong wind in which the snow moves nearly horizontally, and drifting is severe.

BLUSTERY: a wind that changes speed unpredictably, but that is always moderate or strong.

BORA: a cold wind that blows from the north or northeast plains across the lands around the Adriatic Sea. It is most common in spring.

BREEZE: a low-speed wind that can be classified as light, gentle, moderate, fresh, or strong (Beaufort scale 2 to 6).

BUSTER: a sudden, violent, and cold wind that blows from the south across Australia (alternatively referred to in parts of Australia as a "southerly burster" or a

"brickfielder"). It occurs on the eastern side of the Great Diving Range.

CALM: no apparent movement of the air (Beaufort Scale 0).

CALMS: *See* doldrums.

CHINOOK: a foehn type of wind in which moist wind from the Pacific Ocean first moves over the Rocky Mountains, where it loses much of its moisture, then sinks over the frozen plains of the northwestern United States and Canada, warming and drying further as it does so. It often removes several cm/in of snow within a few hours. This is why the chinook is called the "snow-eater." *See* foehn.

CIRCULATION: the way in which air moves within the atmosphere. In general, air moves from regions of high pressure to regions of low pressure, and from places where it is hot to places where it is cold. The spin of the earth makes the flow of air take on curved or spiraling patterns, especially in the midlatitudes.

CLIMATE: the average pattern of the day-to-day weather.

COLD CLIMATES: where there is a long cold season lasting between 6 and 9 months.

CONVECTIONAL RAIN: rain, often torrential, from thunderstorms that have been produced by moist air rising vertically from the surrounding heated land or ocean surface (convectional activity).

COOL TEMPERATE CLIMATES: where the seasons are based on temperature, and where there is a cold season (below 6°C/43°F) of 1 to 5 months. Cool temperate climates can be marine (western margin, with a winter maximum of rain) or continental (eastern margin, with a summer maximum of rain).

COOL TEMPERATE, DRY CLIMATES: dry climates that have hot summers and cold winters. They have an unreliable summer rainfall. They are associated with scrubby vegetation. Steppe, prairie, pampas, and veld are names for midlatitude vegetation zones connected to dry climates. *See* dry climates, cool temperate climates, and steppe.

CYCLONE: a region of rising and inward spiraling air. Air spirals counterclockwise in the northern hemisphere and clockwise in the southern hemisphere. Depressions are weak cyclones, but the term is usually only used for tropical cyclones (hurricanes, typhoons).

DEPRESSION: a midlatitude cyclone or low carried by the westerly winds. Warm, tropical air and cool, polar air are drawn together. The cold, more dense air pushes

below the warm, less dense air. As the warm air rises, it cools, producing broad bands of cloud and rain (or snow). Within a depression air spirals counterclockwise in the northern hemisphere and clockwise in the southern hemisphere.

DESERT CLIMATES/DESERTS: very dry climates in which the amount of precipitation is so low that very little vegetation can grow. Hot deserts are those with no average monthly temperature below 6°C/43°F. Cold deserts are those with at least one cold month. *See* dry climates and hot desert climates.

DISTRIBUTARY: the branch of a river that flows away from the main channel and does not return to it, such as is found on a delta.

DIURNAL: daily.

DOCTOR, THE: a regular, cool onshore wind the blows over a warm coastal area in southwestern Australia. Called the Cape Doctor in southern South Africa.

DOLDRUMS: a zone of calms in the equatorial regions of the world's oceans that moves slightly north or south with the overhead sun. It is associated with daily thunderstorm rain.

DOWNDRAFT: a wind associated with rapid downward movement of air in a thundercloud.

DRY CLIMATES: where the principal feature is that the evaporation and transpiration greatly exceed the precipitation at all times of the year. *See* desert climates, hot dry climates, cool temperate dry climates, and steppe.

DUST DEVIL: a localized spiraling of air on a hot day.

EQUATORIAL CLIMATE: a hot climate, with rain in every month and with two maximum periods of rain just after the time when the overhead sun crosses the equator.

EQUATORIAL LOW: a zone of low-pressure air that encircles the earth in the tropics and whose position is influenced by the overhead sun.

EQUINOX: the two times of the year when the midday sun is overhead at the equator, and the length of day and night is the same everywhere in the world. This happens in March and September.

ETESIAN WIND: a strong northerly wind that blows across Greece and other regions of the eastern Mediterranean.

FOEHN: a warm, dry wind that blows down the leeward side of a mountain, warming as it descends. The name was first used for Alpine valleys, where the wind can be so ferocious that it creates a roaring sound. It is most common in late autumn and in spring.

FRIAGEM: a cold Antarctic wind that blows across southerly regions of South America in the lee of the Andes, and that is associated with the trailing edge of a passing depression (similar to a North American norther or an Australian buster).

GALE: a very strong wind. Gales can be moderate, fresh, or strong (Beaufort scale 7, 8, and 9).

GULF STREAM: a warm ocean current that begins in the Gulf of Mexico and then moves across the surface of the North Atlantic Ocean close to the Atlantic coast of North America before turning east and spreading out to cross the Atlantic Ocean. As soon as it begins to cross the Atlantic Ocean, it is called the North Atlantic Drift.

GUST: a short blast of air.

HABOOB: very strong desert winds usually associated with dust storms in the North African, Arabian, or Indian deserts.

HARMATTAN: a very hot wind that blows southwest from central Africa and can bring clouds of stinging dust.

HEAT WAVE: a few days of unusually hot weather. Heat waves are a feature of the midlatitudes and are normally a result of a tongue of tropical air moving poleward.

HIGH: a region where the air pressure, as measured by a barometer, is higher than average. Highs are places of sinking air and clear, settled weather.

HIGH-PRESSURE SYSTEM: *See* High.

HORSE LATITUDES: the part of the oceans where the winds change from westerly to easterly. They exist near 30°N and 30°S, and create a zone of plentiful sunshine. The world's main deserts lie at the horse latitudes.

HOT CLIMATES: where it is always hot. No month below 18°C/64°F. They are divided into equatorial and tropical types. *See* equatorial climate, tropical marine climate, tropical continental climate, hot dry climates, and tropical monsoon climate.

HOT DESERT CLIMATE: where it is hot and permanently under the influence of trade winds blowing over the land. *See* desert climates.

HOT DRY CLIMATES: dry climates of the tropics and subtropics that may have a short period of unreliable seasonal rain, often associated with a summer monsoon. These regions are characterized by a sparse vegetation of grass and small trees called scrub. The dry savanna is a tropical dry climate vegetation. *See* dry climates and hot climates.

HUMIDITY: the amount of moisture in the air. The full term is relative humidity, which means the amount of moisture in the air compared with the amount that the air could hold. If the relative humidity is close

to the maximum that the air can hold, little moisture evaporates from the skin, and so people feel sticky and uncomfortable.

HURRICANE: a very fierce, damaging wind of the tropics and subtropics. The general term hurricane also refers to a tropical cyclone in North America (Beaufort Scale 12+). *See* tropical cyclone.

HURRICANE FORCE WINDS: winds whose speeds exceed 117kph/73mph.

ICE CLIMATE: a very cold, polar climate with no month above 6°C/43°F. Characterized by permanent ice and frozen ground.

ICELANDIC LOW: the low frequently found over the North Atlantic between Iceland and Greenland, particularly in winter. Represents an area where depressions are frequent.

ISOTHERM: a line joining places with the same temperature. On the maps in this book isotherms are marked by the junctions of different bands of color.

JET STREAM: a tunnel of fast-moving air that normally forms where two different kinds of air meet high in the atmosphere. There are two jet streams in each hemisphere, one near the Arctic/Antarctic circles (called the polar jet stream), the other close to the tropics (called the subtropical jet stream).

KHAMSIN: a hot, dry wind that blows from the Sahara Desert to Egypt. It is known as *rih al khamsin* ("the wind of 50 days") by Egyptians, an indication of how long it lasts.

LEE: the coast or flank of a mountain sheltered from the prevailing winds. The lee side of a mountain is useful as a sheltered harbor, but it may present problems for farming, since lee sides lie in the rainshadow of mountains and so may be quite dry.

LOW: a region in which the air pressure, as measured by a barometer, is lower than average. Lows are places of rising air, cloud, and rain. *See* cyclone, depression.

LOW-PRESSURE SYSTEM: *See* Low.

MEDITERRANEAN CLIMATE: a subtropical climate with a long, dry summer and cool, wet winter. *See* warm temperate climate.

MIDLATITUDES: those parts of the earth that lie between the Tropic of Cancer and the Arctic Circle, and between the Tropic of Capricorn and the Antarctic Circle.

MIDLATITUDE WESTERLY WINDS: *See* prevailing westerly winds.

MISTRAL: a dry and cold wind that blows from the cold Swiss Plateau through the Rhone Valley of France during spring.

MONSOON: any seasonal wind that blows toward a continent in summer and away from it in winter. Used only in connection with places that have distinct wet and dry seasons.

MOUNTAIN CLIMATE: where the temperature is significantly affected by altitude. Usually applies to places above 1,300m/4,000ft.

NORTH ATLANTIC DRIFT: a warm ocean current that flows across the North Atlantic Ocean from the East Coast of North America (where it is called the Gulf Stream) and warms the coasts of northwest Europe. *See* Gulf Stream.

NORTHEASTER, NOR'EASTER: a strong (often gale-force) wind that blows across New England from the northeast.

NORTHER: a cold winter wind that sweeps south from the Canadian prairies across the southern United States and then out over the Gulf of Mexico. It is often pulled south in the rear of passing depressions. A norther may reach a speed of 60kph/40mph, and it often makes the air very dusty.

OVERHEAD SUN: the apparent position of the sun at midday. It is a measure of where the sun's heating is greatest on the earth's surface. The global weather bands are closely related to its position and therefore vary in a predictable way with the seasons.

PACIFIC HIGH: the subtropical high that dominates the Pacific Ocean. Particularly strong in the North Pacific off the West Coast of North America. Stronger in summer than in winter.

PAMPAS: *See* steppe.

PAMPERO: A cold, southerly wind, similar to the norther but occurring east of the Andes in Argentina.

PHOTOCHEMICAL SMOG: *See* smog.

POLAR CLIMATES: very cold climates. *See* ice climate and Arctic climate.

POLAR JET STREAM: a tunnel of very fast-moving air that encircles the earth high in the atmosphere close to the poleward limit of the midlatitudes. It forms into great waves as it moves. These waves influence where depressions and anticyclones will form in the midlatitudes. In general, anticyclones form on parts of the waves that turn down toward the equator, while the part of the wave that turns toward the pole forms strings of depressions.

PRAIRIE: *See* steppe.

PRECIPITATION: all the forms of liquid and solid water that come out of the atmosphere – rain, snow, hail, dew, etc.

PRESSURE: *See* air pressure.

PRESSURE SYSTEMS: the lows (low-pressure systems) and highs (high-pressure systems) in the atmosphere.

PREVAILING WESTERLY WINDS: winds that blow across the midlatitudes from west to east. They contain depressions and anticyclones, and so are associated with changeable weather. Also called westerlies and westerly winds.

RAINSHADOW: a region with relatively low rainfall because it is sheltered from the prevailing winds by mountains or hills. As the winds rise up the windward side of the high land, they cool and release most of their moisture. The now drier winds also warm up as they descend on the lee side, and it is this combination that makes rainfall more scarce. Deserts often lie in the permanent rainshadow regions of the world's highest mountains.

RELIEF RAIN: rain that is the result of moist air being forced to rise as it passes over high land. All winds are capable of producing relief rain as they move from ocean to land, but the amount of rain depends on the height of the relief, and some low-lying areas may therefore get no rain from these winds.

SAHEL: a semiarid region of North Africa between the Sahara Desert and the savannas to the south. Characterized by a short and unreliable wet season and a long dry season. Very prone to drought.

SALINE: salty.

SANTA ANA: a hot, dry wind that flows from the Great Basin between the Sierras and the Rocky Mountains and into the Los Angeles Basin of California, gusting to over 100kph/63mph. It will fan brush-fires.

SAVANNA: natural tropical grasslands with scattered trees and bushes covering large areas of Africa, northern Australia, and South America.

SEA BREEZE: a light wind flowing from the sea onto the land. It forms only during the day. Also called a coastal breeze.

SETTLED WEATHER: where the sky is clear, and sunshine (in warm weather) or fog (in cold weather) is most likely.

SIBERIAN HIGH: the high positioned over north and central Asia in winter.

SIMOOM: the Arabian equivalent of the harmattan wind. Means "poison wind."

SIROCCO: a dry, hot wind from the Sahara that can blow dust and sand across the Mediterranean. Equivalent to the khamsin. It is pulled north into the warm sector of depressions moving through the Mediterranean Sea during autumn and spring. Air temperatures may exceed 40°C/104°F or approach 50°C/122°F.

SMOG: a fog or haze intensified by atmospheric pollution. Smog affected by sunlight is called photochemical smog.

SNOWBIRDS: first coined for people from the northern U.S. who spend the winter in the south each year in order to escape the snow and cold of the north. Also now applies to the seasonal migrations of retired Australians.

SQUALL: a sudden storm of wind with speeds of 40kph/25mph or more and lasting for at least two minutes, typically accompanied by rain, snow, or sleet.

STEPPE: the dry and mostly treeless midlatitude grasslands that occur from central Europe to Siberia in Asia. Steppe is similar to the prairies of North America, the pampas of South America, and the veld of South Africa.

STORM-FORCE WIND: a very strong wind (Beaufort scale 10 and 11).

SUBTROPICAL CLIMATES: See warm temperate climate.

SUBTROPICAL HIGH: a semipermanent region of high-pressure air that forms just poleward of the tropics at the horse latitudes. Such highs form mainly over the oceans and are some of the most durable features of the yearly circulation. Most of these highs have names (e.g., Azores high in the North Atlantic).

SUPERCELLS: regions, usually over the warm oceans near the equator, in which clusters of thunderstorms form and eventually produce tropical cyclones.

TEMPERATE CLIMATES: where the main seasonal changes are due to temperature, but where there is no long, cold winter. See cool temperate climate and warm temperate climate.

TEMPERATURE: the amount of heat present, measured using a thermometer and shown by a scale such as °C (degrees Celsius) or °F (degrees Fahrenheit). Weather reports normally give the temperature of the air measured in the shade.

THERMAL: a rising spiral of warm air.

TORNADO: an extremely violent, tightly spiraling column of air that reaches down from the bottom of a giant thunderstorm.

TORNADO WATCH: a government observation network designed to give warning of tornadoes.

TRADE WINDS: winds that blow constantly from the subtropical highs toward the equator. In the northern hemisphere the trade winds blow from the northeast (northeast trade winds). In the southern hemisphere they blow from the southeast (southeast trade winds). They tend to bring rain when they blow onto an easterly coast and drought when they blow off a westerly coast.

TRANSPIRATION: the release of water vapor into the air by plants as they respire.

TROPICAL CONTINENTAL CLIMATE: a hot climate with no month below 18°C/64°F. Dry seasons occur at the time when the trade winds blow, and wet seasons of thundery weather correspond with the influence of the equatorial low.

TROPICAL CYCLONE: a severe low-pressure region that originates in the tropics, and that develops spiraling hurricane-force winds. Tropical cyclones are called hurricanes in the Americas and typhoons in the North Pacific.

TROPICAL MARINE CLIMATE: a hot climate in which the trade winds bring rain for part of the year, and in which the equatorial low dominates for the rest of the year, bringing calm weather but daily thunderstorms. Mainly affects tropical islands.

TROPICAL MONSOON CLIMATE: a hot climate with no month below 18°C/64°F, and in which the wet season corresponds to a time when moist air flows onshore from the neighboring hot ocean. Monsoon climates have higher rainfalls than those that simply experience an ordinary wet season.

TROPICS: the part of the earth that lies between the Tropic of Cancer (22.5°N) and the Tropic of Capricorn (22.5°S).

TWISTER: a tornado.

TYPHOON: a hurricane that occurs in the Pacific Ocean.

VELD, VELDT: See steppe.

WADI: a term of Arabic origin for a gorge that is dry except during flash floods.

WARM TEMPERATE CLIMATES: a climate in which there is rain at all times of the year, and in which there are seasons based on temperature, but in which there is no cold season (no month below 6°C/43°F). Also sometimes called subtropical climate. Warm temperate climates on the eastern coasts of continents have a rainfall maximum in summer; those on the western coasts have a maximum in winter and are also called Mediterranean climates. Warm temperate climates can also experience monsoon effects.

WEATHER: the nature of the atmosphere as we experience it each day.

WEATHER HAZARD: conditions that put the lives and property of people at risk. They include heavy rain causing landslides and floods, hurricanes, tornadoes, and droughts.

WESTERLIES: See prevailing westerly winds.

WESTERLY WINDS: See prevailing westerly winds.

WILLY-WILLY: a tropical cyclone that occurs in the seas north and west of Australia.

WINDCHILL: the added effect of a strong, cold wind on the rate of heat loss from the body.

WINDWARD: the coast or flank of a mountain facing the prevailing winds. Windward coasts not only have frequent strong winds, but also, since the air is forced to rise over the land, it cools and releases its moisture as cloud and rain. As a result, windward areas usually have plentiful rain. Relief effects are important with both the trade winds and the midlatitude westerlies.

Set Index

USING THIS INDEX

This index covers all 12 volumes in the *WeatherWatch* set:

Volume number	Title
1:	January
2:	February
3:	March
4:	April
5:	May
6:	June
7:	July
8:	August
9:	September
10:	October
11:	November
12:	December

An example entry:
Index entries are listed alphabetically.

Calcutta **1–12**: 35; **9**: *36–37*

Volume numbers are in bold and are followed by page references. Entire articles on a subject are shown by italic page numbers. (The "Quick reference" section is on page 2, and the "Glossary" is on pages 44–46.)
In the example above, "Calcutta" appears in all 12 volumes on page 35 and as a full article on pages 36 and 37 of Volume 9: September.

47